The Essential Guide to

Wedding Planning

Expert Advice and Tips for Your Perfect Wedding

Karly Valentine

Professional Wedding Consultant

The Essential Guide to Wedding Planning

Expert Advice and Tips for Your Perfect Wedding

Copyright

ISBN-13: 978-1516987573

ISBN-10: 1516987578

Disclaimer

The publisher and the author make no representation or warranties with respect to the accuracy or completeness of the contents of this work and specifically disclaim all warranties, including without limitation warranties of fitness for a particular purpose. No warranty may be created or extended by sales or promotional materials. The advice and strategies contained herein may not be suitable for every situation. This work is solid with the understanding that neither the publisher nor the author is engaged in rendering legal, accounting, or other professional services. If professional assistance is required, the services of a competent professional person should be sought. Neither the publisher nor the author shall be liable for damages arising here from. The fact that an organization or website is referenced in this work as a citation and/or a potential source of further information does not mean that the author or the publisher endorses the information the organization or website may provide or recommendations it may make. Further, readers should be aware that internet websites listed in this work may have changed or disappeared between the date this work was written and when it is read.

Table of Contents

WEEDING & GIFT REGISTRY

Your Guide to A Perfect Wedding Registry

Wedding Registry Etiquette that Every Couple Should Know

The Wedding Registry Must Haves

HONEYMOON

Honeymoon Planning

Types of Honeymoons

Whether or Not you should Use a Travel Agent

Budgeting - Know Your Budget and How to Save

How to Choose the Location

Popular Destinations

Honeymoon Accommodations

Activities

Making Reservations

Making Memories

To Do List

SAYING THANK YOU

Saying Thank You after Your Wedding

Thank You Cards

WEDDING PLANNING APPS

Apps That Make Your Wedding Planning Easier

ADDITIONAL THINGS TO KEEP IN MIND

Stress! Stress! Stress!

The Bridezilla Mindset

GETTING STARTED

Introduction

Planning a wedding is not an easy task. There is a lot to consider, and many people go the route of hiring someone who will help them to take care of it all. Whether you choose this option or not, there is a long road with many decisions ahead of you. Your wedding may be the single most expensive day in your life, and will hopefully be the happiest and most memorable. For this reason, it is important that you get it right. This pressure adds more difficulty to the task of planning it, leaving you feeling frustrated and stressed for the whole process.

There are many things to consider, and it may be that you have not yet thought of them all. Here we can give you some advice on all of the things that you need to think about, from the big decisions such as venue, down to smaller things such as your something borrowed. Whether you are doing it alone or with help, this guide will help you to navigate your way through the many aspects of wedding planning that must be negotiated before the big day. The most important thing is not to panic – take a deep breath, read our advice, and dive in.

The big thing that you have to remember throughout all of this is that you are getting married because you love each other. You are ready to spend the rest of your lives together and be a family. All of this can sometimes get a bit lost in the middle of the chaos and stress of planning.

Let's consider the story of two different couples. One of them is able to get everything organized well ahead of time. They have everything in place months before the wedding, and a schedule which tells them what to do and when. Now let's consider the story of another couple, who like to play things by ear. They do not plan ahead, but instead plan to arrange each part of the wedding as it comes.

What do you think happens to these two couples? The first one will, of course, get everything sorted out and ready for the big day. It might be that a few things do not quite go to plan, but of course that is alright, because they already have a contingency plan in place, which allows them to take care of such things.

But what about the second couple? Things do not go so well for them. They do not get their bookings made in time, and so in a few areas, they have to end up making compromises on what they really wanted. Then, of course, there are a few things they did not plan for at all. As a result, they end up going over their budget. By the time that they make it down the aisle, they are wondering whether they can really afford to go on their honeymoon. Being prepared will help to prevent this situation.

Throughout this book, we will cover a range of topics that will guide you through all of your wedding plans from start to finish. We'll begin by looking at setting the date and choosing a location. We will also help you to decide whether you may need a wedding planning consultant or not, and whether you should try to DIY your wedding. If you do go down this route, we have plenty of tips on ways to make this work.

After this we will look at your budget, which is one of the most essential parts of the wedding planning. You can figure out how much your wedding will cost, who should pay for what, and how to save some money. We'll discuss the engagement, how it works, and how to plan a wedding party, as well. When your engagement celebrations are over, it's time to dive into the wedding planning.

We can give you a schedule so that you are able to get all of your wedding planning done within the right timeframe. This means starting with the here and now, and moving all the way up to the day before the ceremony. The ceremony itself leaves a lot to be considered. We'll look at styles and themes, writing your vows, choosing an officiate, creating a ceremony that suits you, and even choosing the wedding rings. The whole wedding party will be considered, as well as all decorations and how you record the ceremony. You will have a to-do list which tells you what is needed and when.

You'll build your wedding party, and then we can move on to deciding on the dress. This is a huge thing to think about, but we also need to consider the groom and his outfit. The bridesmaids and groomsmen will also come into it. We will sort out flowers for everyone, and then start heading on to the reception planning.

We'll pick out a location, sort out seating plans, choose a caterer and food menu, and sort out the drinks. We will tackle the wedding cake, and then sort out your gift registry so that you get exactly what you need. Soon we'll be on to the honeymoon, and all of the planning that is required for that before you even get to the wedding.

Just in case you need some help with organizing everything, we will look at some wedding planning apps that will sort you out with the best possible results. We can also give you some advice that might make you feel better about this whole planning process. We'll reassure you about the myths surrounding weddings, and the emotions that you are bound to experience. We will tell you how to plan a wedding even when it feels difficult. Finally, we'll show you how to not only survive your wedding – but to truly enjoy it.

By the end of this book, you should be ready to tackle wedding planning and create your perfect day. So what are you waiting for? Let's get started!

WEDDING: The Most Memorable and Expensive Day of Your Life

Planning a wedding is not an easy task. There is a lot to consider, and many people go the route of hiring someone who will help them to take care of it all. Whether you choose this option or not, there is a long road with many decisions ahead of you. Your wedding may be the single most expensive day in your life, and will hopefully be the happiest and most memorable. For this reason, it is important that you get it right. This pressure adds more difficulty to the task of planning it, leaving you feeling frustrated and stressed with the whole process.

There are many things to consider, and it may be that you have not yet thought of them all. Here we can give you some advice on all of the things that you need to think about, from the big choices such as venue, down to smaller things such as your something borrowed. Whether you are doing it alone or with help, this guide will help you to navigate your way through the many aspects of wedding planning that must be negotiated before the big day. The most important thing is not to panic – take a deep breath, read our advice, and dive in.

The big thing that you have to remember throughout all of this is that you are getting married because you love each other. You are ready to spend the rest of your lives together and be a family. All of this can sometimes get a bit lost in the middle of the chaos and stress of planning. It is very likely that you are going to have a few arguments during this process, perhaps big enough that you consider cancelling the wedding. Believe it or not, this is actually perfectly natural and happens to a lot of couples. Everything gets on top of you, and the result is that you take it out on each other.

It's almost inevitable that these fights will come, but take a deep breath when you feel like shouting and see if you can talk things over. If you need your partner to give more input, explain to them that you need to feel as though they care as much as you do. If you have too much on your plate, ask them to help out. Hopefully you can straighten things out. But if you do get into that screaming match, afterwards it is important to remember why you are doing all of this.

After the dust has settled, take the time to let your partner know that you love them and you are still committed to your relationship. Let them know that you only get angry because you care so much about getting your big day right. Once all is forgiven, you can start again, and perhaps things will go more smoothly. Remember to have each other's backs. If your partner is starting to look too stressed, help them out!

Wedding Planning Tips and Etiquette

There are some things that you need to get firmly in your mind right away, so be sure to focus on these. The biggest tip that we can give you is to plan everything very carefully. Timing is essential here because you have a deadline to work towards. Your first and most important job is to choose that date – and to be realistic about it. If it is too soon, then you may not be able to organize everything in time. Once you have the date in place you can start to think about everything else that needs to be done.

Etiquette is also something that you need to take into consideration. The general rule is this: be polite, be considerate, and follow the rules. This means that you should be careful about your decisions. It is alright to have a wedding that is out of the ordinary, but some lines should not be crossed if you can help it. For example, it is considered bad etiquette to hold a wedding in the middle of the week. A weekend is very easy to organize, but on a Wednesday, your guests will all need to take some time off work to attend. They might not be very happy about that!

Generally speaking, you should try to maintain a clear but honest approach. Many people might ask unexpected things or put you into a difficult position. The correct etiquette is to deal with them firmly, rather than stringing them along. The classic example is of someone who wants to know when they will receive their invite – not realizing that you have no plans to include them. You might feel the need to avoid an awkward situation, and to tell them that you just haven't got around to it yet. This will only lead to further problems in the future when they still have not received their invitation. You should tell them that you are keeping the guest list small and restricted only to those closest to the family, as this is a diplomatic answer that will only upset them for a moment. It prevents the issue from being dragged out.

When it comes to finances, etiquette normally dictates that guests pay their own way. If they need to stay in a hotel or travel to you, they should pay for this themselves. That goes for bridesmaids and groomsmen, too. If you have spare money or you are supporting family members, then you can choose to pay for them. However, it is certainly not expected. You should perhaps get a gift for your bridesmaids and groomsmen, though. This can be something they can wear on the day, or a general gift you know they will appreciate. This is to say thank you to them for making the effort to help you out. It's a great idea to read up on attendant's etiquette a bit further. For example, you can have your parents be your attendants if you do not want bridesmaids and groomsmen.

How to Set the Dates

There are a few important dates that you need to decide on as soon as possible. The first to come will be your engagement party, if you are going to have one. Then you will have your stag and hen nights, or bachelor parties. After this will be the wedding itself – which you will want to work out first so you can organize the rest around it – and then your honeymoon. These dates need to be set carefully because if they clash with something else, you may find that you lose half your dates.

Your first consideration for your wedding date may well be your venue. If you already have a dream venue in mind, then you will need to see which dates they have available. If you are more flexible, you can look around a little bit and see which dates are available in general before you decide. You may even choose between two venues by seeing which dates they can make. It is essential that you have a venue, because otherwise you are not going to be able to get married. Although everyone will be asking you when you will set the date, stay calm and put him or her off. You can announce the date only once you have finally settled on and booked the venue.

An engagement typically lasts from six months up to a year and a half, but can be longer. If your dream venue is fully booked for two years, there is nothing wrong with waiting until you can get it. If you want to get married faster, you might have some trouble, as the venues are likely to be booked up. You should also think about the season you would prefer, as well as trying to avoid big events. These may include family birthdays or events, holidays, and even sporting events that you know everyone will want to watch or attend.

Try not to rush yourself – picking an early date will not leave you enough time to plan everything. Just take it slowly. Unless you have a very good reason to get married quickly, it's better to delay a little to ensure that everything will be perfect. You do not have to take your honeymoon right away if the dates are not suitable for you. For modern weddings, it is becoming more and more acceptable to see couples taking a break between the wedding and their honeymoon in order to cope with work or family responsibilities. For your bachelor and bachelorette, avoid the night before the wedding, as this can lead to hangovers on the day (and you will probably need to attend a rehearsal dinner). Leave around two or three days before the wedding before having the party. This makes it easier to recover and get back to last minute planning before the big day. The engagement party can be held as soon as you like – or left a way off if you feel that you need a little time to plan.

The Venue: Finding the Perfect Location

The venue that you choose for your wedding is a huge decision – perhaps even the biggest thing that you will have to look at. It will influence the date that you choose, and will have an impact on your budget and your guest list. The catering facilities available will affect your menu, and it will all determine how your wedding photos will look, as many shots will be taken here. You have to consider both your wedding ceremony and your reception. Think about travelling between them as well, as your guests will have to make that journey with you.

There are plenty of factors that will influence your decision. First of all, think about how many people you are likely to invite. This is not a finalized headcount, but more of an estimate. You need to get this right because it will influence the amount of room that you need. Find out how much space is there from the venue owners, and then think about whether it will be enough. Having a space that is too small just will not do – you will have to cut people from the invite list that you actually wanted there. You also need to look at the logistics: there should be areas set out where people can eat, drink, chat, and dance. Not having room for all of these activities might make the party fall a bit flat.

You may want to consider privacy levels, as well. If you are in a more public place, then you may have strangers coming past your group. They may even be able to come in or take photographs from outside. If you are not comfortable with this, then you need a venue with some level of privacy. You may even want to have your location booked exclusively, so that only your guests should be on site.

Look at the lighting, too. A nighttime reception will require plenty of electric lighting, enough so that you can see your food and the faces of your guests at minimum. If it is during the day, then big windows might be a great option. Test out the space during the time that you want to book it. It may look different under different lights. The best example of this is a threadbare carpet − which may look great under candlelight, but awful in full daylight.

Alongside these thoughts, you might also consider the outdoor area where you will most likely have some professional photographs taken. Think about the coloring of the room as well, and whether it will match your theme. You may need to find a lot of electrical outlets if you are bringing lots of entertainment. Acoustics should be taken into account in the event that the room is too echoed, or you can hear a lot of noise from outside. Parking also needs to be considered unless you are planning to organize a bus for your guests.

Should You Hire a Wedding Planner?

This is a burning question for many engaged couples. It seems like there is so much to organize on your own – perhaps too much. But if you are going to hire someone else to help you out, your budget will take a hit. So what is the right thing to do?

Here we can discuss some of the options so that you are able to make the right decision. There is no one definitive answer – it depends on many factors, and each individual couple should make the decision for themselves.

Let's start by looking at what wedding planners do. If you can tick off most of these things as being something you need help with, then hiring someone might be a great choice. They will work on a realistic budget with you, which take into account your funds as well as what is needed to achieve the vision you have in mind. They will create a master plan for the wedding that covers everything from the big picture to the little details, so that everything can be planned and organized in time. They will find a location for you, even scouting venues themselves for your consideration. They can also help to find local vendors in your price range, such as florists, photographers and videographers, catering teams, bands or DJs, and other entertainment.

They may also be able to save you some money through the vendors that they have special relationships with. If you cannot save money, you may at least get some extras thrown in for free. They will look over contracts with these vendors on your behalf to ensure that you are covered in case of cancelations. They can create schedules for anyone involved with the wedding so they know what to do in the run up to the day, and on the day itself. They can take care of invitations for you so that all you have to do is come up with your guest list. They can help a lot on the wedding day to organize everything as it happens.

They can even advise you on what should and should not be done, or what kinds of trends are currently happening in the wedding scene. They can actually help beyond the big day too, preparing your honeymoon plans and taking care of booking everything on your behalf.

You can do all of these things yourself if you spend a lot of time working on them. If you only work part time or spend your days at home, you may well be able to pull it off easily. On the other hand, you can do it when you are working full time as well – but be prepared to give up most if not all of your free time to think about it. Taking the stress off your shoulders is a great reason to hire a planner. Saving money is a great reason not to.

DOING IT YOURSELF

DIY Tips for an Affordable Wedding

If you are thinking about taking on some or all of the elements of your wedding yourself, it's important first to think about the reasons behind it. We have to make this point because so many people are catching on to the trend of DIY weddings at the moment. The question you need to ask yourself is if you think that it is realistic that you really can create your dream wedding under your own efforts. If you would have better luck with professionals, and you are probably going to end up tearing your hair out, then maybe you could try to save costs another way.

It is essential that you examine your intentions and to know your goals before you start. It is easy to get sucked in to Pinterest guides that tell you how easy it is to do everything you need! Unfortunately, this may not always be the case. If your sole aim is to save money, then be wary. By the time you have purchased all of the equipment and materials you need, wasted some of it through beginner mistakes, and ended up with an inferior finished product, you may not save much money at all. In fact, it is completely possible to follow one of these tutorials and then find that you have actually spent more than you would have if you just hired a planner in the first place.

Remember that those who put together tutorials are normally very well versed in the methods they need already. They have perhaps tried making these items or decorations several times already before reaching the finished product you see online. Consider also that if you are relying on your guests to do things for you, you may be let down. They may not be interested in helping, may not have the skills, or might just have a few too many drinks as the reception continues on.

If your goal is to personalize your wedding as much as possible, then this is a good reason to get started. Rather than focusing on cost, it shows that you are thinking about each other and of having a wedding that is not perfect, but rather personal. With this idea in mind, you can DIY some elements of the wedding but leave others to the professionals. This is a much more reasonable approach because it means that you can take care of what is possible rather than scrambling to do everything. Keep in mind that the stress of making everything will be added to the initial stress of organizing it, and this can make the burden on your shoulders that much heavier.

Still, if you are positive about the idea of a DIY wedding, then go ahead and get started. The sooner you begin planning, the better. You can achieve a lot if you give yourself enough time. Don't be afraid to delegate, either – friends and family may be a valuable resource that you can use wisely.

You Can Do It Together

If you decide to go the DIY route, then it is important that you share the jobs amongst the two of you. Marriage is something that you enter into as a couple, and leave as one single unit. This is all about joining the two of you together. With that in mind, it should start as a joint venture – not an attempt to create something on your own. Even if one of you is more skilled in making things or has all of the ideas that does not mean that it should be a solo attempt. The effort needs to come from both of you.

You both need to give your soul to this project, because it is something that needs to be heartfelt and sincere. If you do everything as quickly as possible without putting any effort into it, and just follow instructions rather than customizing, you will find that your wedding does not have a big impact. The spirit of DIT, or Do-It-Together, is all about capturing the essence of yourselves and your relationship. You need to make something that your friends and family will recognize as being true to yourselves. This is how you can make your day perfect and memorable without having to purchase or hire everything readymade.

As an added bonus, working together will give you some extra time to bond, and prevent a falling out. You may well get a little ratty with one another after weeks of working on seemingly fiddly projects that just keep going wrong. But when you have the finished product in your hands, you will feel pride in each other for the hours spent on getting it right. You will feel closer as a couple, and ready to walk hand in hand into married life. If one person were to do all of the work on his or her own, trouble may arise. You might feel that your other half is leaving you with all of the work and responsibility while they contribute nothing. On the other hand, they might feel as though you are taking over and not letting them have any input.

It may well be that you are able to do most of the work (or your other half is) without causing any disputes. The way to handle this is to make sure that you are both involved in every part of the decision making process. You can both have a creative input on which areas you DIY, how you do it, what colors you choose, and so on. There is no need to take over everything just because the other person is busy or doesn't know much about DIY. You should share this process in order to DIT, and create a lasting foundation for your marriage.

Collaborating in this way also ensures that you are both happy on the day itself. All areas of wedding planning often require compromise, but the solution should be one that you both agree on. If only one of you likes the decor, you have gone wrong somewhere.

DIY Ideas

There are some things that it can be very easy to DIY. The first thing that you need to think about is your own skills and resources. Being practical means thinking about what you are actually able to achieve. This depends on your budget, your time, and your ability. Keep that in mind all the way through the process of deciding what to DIY. You can enlist friends and family to help, but remember that they should be rewarded for doing something for you. Just roping them in and taking them for granted may cause bad blood. It's better to think about getting them a gift or exchanging their help for yours later on.

One area that you might be able to DIY successfully and at low cost is your hair and makeup. Everyone has at least one friend who is really great at makeovers, and this could be their chance to help you out. You can even learn how to do it yourself from videos on YouTube or tutorials on Pinterest. The practical way to get this done is to practice as much as you can before the day. You can also purchase a few key pieces of make up or equipment to help you out. The good news is that you will be able to use them after the wedding too. Wedding make up tends to be quite natural and simple, so you might be able to get away with it so long as you have some experience in doing it yourself.

Decorating your ceremony venue yourself is also a really practical idea. You will only be in there for a short while and then will head off to your reception venue, so it does not need to look perfect. Saving money here could give you a lot more to spend on the arrangements for the evening. If the site is pretty enough as it is, then you might be able to get away with minimal decorations. Having some flowers on display or just lighting candles around the venue might do the job. Candles are especially great because you can take them home afterwards and use them later.

Creating invitations yourself is also a great idea, and in some ways it can even said to be a fashion. You can personalize each invitation just by going to a local paper or craft store and picking up a few packs of paper. You can hand-write them, and then spend some time gluing on extra frills and ribbons if you want. Keep the invites to a smaller size if you can, as this will cost less to post. A handwritten invitation can make a bigger impact and appear to be more special for those who receive them. Just make sure that you get started ahead of the time when you want to send them out. A few hand cramps might get in your way if you have a long list of guests!

Flowers

If you want to sort out your wedding flowers yourself, then you might need a lot of patience and some knowhow from the experts. Thankfully there are countless tutorials online that you can watch if you wish to, so there should be plenty of inspiration out there for you. Most likely you will want to focus on a bouquet for the bride, buttonholes for the groom and groomsmen, and perhaps some table favors to decorate your reception area. We can give you some quick tips on sorting those out here. The first thing to note is that you should try to use hardy flowers that do not mind being handled. Roses are a great example, and miniature calla lilies may work for the buttonholes.

To make your bouquet, you should ideally have between 30 and 60 stems, while a bridesmaid bouquet will need only 20 to 40. You will want a bucket to keep them in, paper towels, rubber bands, a very sharp knife, and straight pins. You may also want to invest in a stem stripper and cutter. The final touch will be a ribbon in a color that matches your scheme, of around 1 or 2 inches in width. When you begin, you will want to take off any leaves or thorns from the stems, and also pull out any petals that are damaged or wilting. Put them back into your bucket of water and then cut the stems at an angle about two inches away from their end. You should do this underwater to help them last longer.

Leave them in the water for a few seconds, and then put them into another bucket that is only halfway filled with cool water until you are ready. Put four flowers together in a square shape at an even height; now arrange all of the other flowers around them one by one. They should be at slightly different heights so that you end up with a dome shape. Now use a rubber band to tie them exactly where they all join together. Do the same thing about two inches above the bottom of the stems. Cut them all to the same length and dry them on your paper towels. Finally, tuck your ribbon into the top bind and then wrap it around the full length of the stems. Secure it with the pins at the end.

Creating a centerpiece is a very similar process, except without the last step. Just trim them to the height required by your vase and settle them in water. For buttonholes, once the flowers are prepared, cut them to three inches long. Get a leaf and tuck it behind the flower, then put a six inches long piece of wire behind them. Wrap floral tape around the stems to secure them, and then cut again to around one and a half inches. Curl the end around a pencil and pinch it to finish off. Finally, use pins to secure it to the lapel.

Music

Booking entertainment for the occasion can be very pricey. Some people choose to go with a live DJ, while others will hire a band. But what if your budget is restricted? You may well be able to set up a scenario where you can DJ your wedding yourself – but it will require a volunteer to look after the tunes and the right venue first. This is a risky idea because it can easily end up going awry, so we have included some warning signs to look out for.

The first point to make is that you will need a sound system in place in your venue. Most reception venues will have speakers that you can plug into in order to play music around the whole location. If there is no sound system in place, then you will need to think about renting one. By the time that you have done that, you might find that it is easier just to find a local DJ. If there is a sound system in place, however, you may be in luck. The easiest option is to get an MP3 player such as an iPod hooked up to the speakers, and then you will be ready to dance all night long.

Remember that you are going to be restricted to only the music that you have on this iPod, so it is a really good idea to prepare it before the day. You might not have the same tastes as all of your guests, but they will no doubt find it a little grating to only be able to listen to the music that you like. Try downloading some playlists or compilation albums to help to bridge the gap between their interests and yours. This will help to get a fresher feeling and give everything something to enjoy.

You can start the music early on once everyone has finished eating, or right away if you are having a more casual buffet approach. It's important to start out with light, easy songs, as not everyone will be on their feet just yet. They will be eating and drinking, chatting, and waiting for someone to take the first plunge. Traditional wedding mixes might be a good idea here, or even recorded string quartet versions. A little later on you can bring in the more up to date music. When everyone is ready to dance, it is appropriate to choose modern songs that are currently in the charts.

The problem that you will have is that a live DJ would assess the mood of the crowd to decide when to play each song.

They would also be able to take requests and change things up when required. To help with this, you can set up a number of different playlists. A member of your wedding party can change between them when it is felt to be appropriate. This will help with the atmosphere.

Photography

Wedding photography can be one of your biggest expenses, and of course you will want to capture every moment of the day. But what happens if you cannot stretch your budget far enough? You may be able to get hold of student photographers who will do it at a lower price, but this is never guaranteed. It may well be that you just do not have enough budget left to stretch even to that. In this case, you might have to get creative in order to get a permanent memory of your big day down on paper.

One of the most popular ideas is to get single-use film cameras as table favors. This gives everyone around the table the chance to take some snaps of their own, allowing you to crowd source your reception photos. There are a few things to be wary of here, however. First is that the store that develops your photos may mess up and ruin the films, leaving you with nothing. Second is that you have no guarantee that everyone will be taking pictures of the right things. What's most likely is that the children will get hold of them and run around taking pictures of whatever they like. Unless you have a plan ready for how to get your guests snapping at the right times, you may wish to proceed very carefully.

Another way to do it is to ask that all of your guests bring their own digital camera or camera phone. You can create a Facebook page for your wedding where everyone can upload their shots, or just ask them to send everything over in an email when they get the chance. If you are familiar with DropBox, you can use this service to store photos and create folders that other people can easily add to. This will make an easy solution to get hundreds, if not thousands, of images all in one place. It's a great idea to specifically focus on anyone in your family who has experience as a photographer or an artist as they are likely to get the best shots.

You can coordinate easily by having cheeky homemade signs around your venue. For example, have the maid of honor or best man hold up a "cameras please!" sign at moments that you want to capture. This can be done in a very fun way and will make the guests feel as though they are really involved. The important thing is getting all of your shots in the same place after the day has finished. Some people might be very slow in getting them back to you. If this is the case, be sure to send them reminders and even offer to come and pick up the memory card to transfer them to your computer. Once they realize how serious you are about getting hold of the photos, they will hand them over and let you complete your collection.

Self-Catering

Most people would hear the words "self-catering" and run for the hills. Organizing food for a whole wedding party of people seems like an insane task. But on the other hand, that it might be easier and a lot more doable than you think. There are a few factors that might grant you success if you manage to get them right. It may seem like nothing short of a miracle would be needed to pull it off but that is just not the case. Let's take a look here at some of the things that you will need to get it done to a good standard.

One factor that might make it possible is a small wedding party. If you have opted to create a small gathering for family and close friends only, then your guests may not number in the hundreds. This will allow you an opportunity, thanks to the fact that a smaller amount of people will require less food. You can always get around the problem of serving by putting things in a buffet format, and that opens the way for a lot of things to be bought in as well. Crisps can be bought in packets and simply placed in bowls, and finger food elements like mini sausages can be given the same treatment. It's only on elements like sandwiches and hot food that you need to coordinate a bit more.

Another factor that will work in your favor is if you have someone in the family who is good at cooking, and accustomed to doing it on a large scale. This is most likely to be one of the mothers, or an aunt who has catered to family gatherings before. They should be able to organize enough hot food to suit the needs of a small party by going for small and simple dishes. The key is just to stick to cold food as much as possible and only have a few hot dishes. They need to be served warm so whoever helps out is going to end up missing part of the reception – you need to make sure that they are fine with this.

The alternative is to make all of your food cold. This may or may not go over well with guests. If you plan your wedding for the middle of the summer on a hot day, then they may not have a problem at all. If it is the middle of winter, however, they will ideally want something to warm themselves up. Think about this carefully before you get started.

Finally, you need to consider the wedding cake. You can absolutely practice making it before the day – perhaps make your own engagement party cake and prepare some for other big family events such as birthdays. This will get your baking skills up to par. It is very important to get the cake right; otherwise you may feel as though you have ruined the day. You might consider buying the cake professionally, if nothing else.

Together We Can

The thing about your wedding is that it is a bond made between the two of you. You are making a promise to stick together forever, through thick and thin, through whatever hardships may come. You are affirming your love to the world and creating a physical representation of that in the form of your rings. Planning and organizing a wedding is very similar in description. You may work through hardships, such as difficulties with organization or trouble with double-booked venues. You will argue and then come back together because of your bond of love. At the end of it all, your wedding will stand as a testament to the depth of the feelings that you have for one another.

The great thing about doing a DIY or DIT wedding is that you will both have put in the effort needed to make your wedding work. This is a very necessary part of preparing your life together. You will of course be planning together and making decisions if you choose to hire vendors instead of going the DIY route, but your work will be on more of a mental than a physical level in this case.

The decisions that you make and the way that you make them could lay the foundations of your marriage. For example, imagine that you are not able to come to a decision or compromise on the table favors. You want floral arrangements, while your other half wants a modern take with vintage items. Neither of you is willing to back down. How do you resolve the situation? The way that you act now could reflect on other decisions in the future. It might affect the way that you choose your child's name, or where they go to school. It might have a bearing on your future house or where you live. This is a time when you learn how to make the hard decisions together, rather than butting heads until one of you backs down.

It's also a very good time for both of you to explore the way that you feel about one another, too. Most likely you will find that your love goes deeper and has more strength than you ever knew. Arriving at the final destination of the wedding day itself may seem like a dream. Long days and nights of tearing your hair out will seem like a thing of the past. All that will matter on the day is how perfect it all is – and it will be perfect, because you love one another.

Remember that this labor of love will have that fantastic ending when it feels as though it is all too much. There will surely be times when you almost feel that you need to give up. At these times, take a deep breath, and go and sit with your partner. Remember how much you love them. This will help you to regain your focus.

BUDGETING FOR THE WEDDING

Budgeting

One of the main areas of concern for your wedding will be the budget. The amount of money that you can afford to spend will have an impact on how big or extravagant your wedding can be. You have to think about it as one of the earliest possible considerations – do not even book a venue unless you know how much money you have to spend. You could end up wasting money by losing your deposit if you have to cancel to free up some more room for other things. In this chapter, we will be showing you how to set up and manage a budget properly.

There are many things that you have to fund. The ceremony itself will require a venue, as well as someone to officiate the marriage. You will need to get a marriage license as well as pay other assorted fees that are required. Then you also need to think about what you wear – buying or renting dresses and tuxedos, along with the bridesmaids and groomsmen's outfits. You may not always pay for these yourself – but we will get on to who pays what a little later on. Flowers will be needed including the bride's bouquet and the groom's buttonhole, as well as any corsages and decorations.

The reception is likely to be the most costly part of the whole event, perhaps bar your honeymoon. This is where the majority of your individual expenses will come in. You need a venue, and that venue needs to be decorated. You need to provide food for your guests as well as entertainment. You may also need to think about transportation from the ceremony to the reception if guests would not be able to travel there themselves. Drinks are also a consideration. Again, this might be something that your guests can pay for themselves rather than taking it out of your budget.

Alongside all of this, you will most likely want to have a photographer and perhaps also a videographer to document the event for you. They will make sure that everything is recorded and that you can relive your day later on. They may well be the source of extra costs later on, such as if you decide to get more prints made or a larger wedding album. Your pre-wedding costs are important to consider, too. A bachelor and bachelorette party can be expensive. Do not forget to send out invites to everyone, as well as save-the-date cards if you decide on a date before everything else is confirmed.

Don't forget the rings, either! This is a very important part of your budget because you will be wearing these rings for the rest of your life. You do not want to skimp on them. Make sure that you have enough money set aside to get rings that are well fitted and that suit your personalities. When all of that is sorted, you still have the honeymoon to book and pay for before you are finished.

How Much Will it Cost?

This is a question that is something along the lines of "how long is a piece of string", because every wedding is different. It actually depends on what you are willing to spend and what kind of wedding you want to have. Some factors will push the costs up, so watch out for those if you want to save money. As a general rule, you can say that 150 people coming to your wedding should have an average cost of about $25,000. This will, of course, be higher in urban areas, where hiring a venue will cost more.

What you really have to consider is how much each part of your wedding will cost. The idea is to think about how much is the maximum you can afford, and then set a budget a little below that. Whatever you plan will always come out over budget in the end, so do not plan to use up all of the money that you have set aside. Leave a little spare just in case. Now that you have your overall budget, you can divide it up to see what different costs should be for your wedding.

Around fifty percent of your budget, and no less than 48 percent, is going to be spent on your reception. This is a big cost because of the logistics involved. You need the venue, decorations, servers, and food for all of your guests. It will cost a lot. That, unfortunately, is the way it is! Next you will spend only two or three percent on the ceremony, because it is one of the quickest parts of the day and you only really need a venue, license, and adjudicate. Your clothing, as in the wedding dress and groom's tux, will take between eight and ten percent of the budget. The same amount should be set aside for entertainment and music on the day. You might need a little more, perhaps ten to twelve percent, for your photographer or videographer. Stationary – primarily invitations – will cost just two to three percent of the budget, as will the wedding rings, and parking or transportation for you. Gifts for those who have helped out and your wedding party will be around the same amount, as well. Finally, all of the other expenses that do not fit into these categories might cost around eight percent.

Of course, all of this has been established without mentioning the honeymoon. If you are paying for it yourself, then make sure to set aside another budget for that, within reasonable bounds. Otherwise, see if you can request funds as your wedding gift from one or the other of your families. It may well be that they can pay for the honeymoon and take the weight off your shoulders. This will give you a little more room to work on your wedding budget and get everything that you want, even if money is tight.

Who Pays For What?

This is one of the biggest questions when it comes to organizing a wedding, and unfortunately it can be one of the most awkward. No one likes to talk about money, but in this case, it may be time to start thinking about who pays for what. Let's note first of all that there is no real need to stick to the traditional structure these days. More and more couples are able to pay for everything themselves. However, we will review the traditional system here so that you can determine whether it would suit you.

The ceremony should be the financial responsibility of the bride and her family when it comes to arranging the church or other venue, as well as an organist, if required. The groom's family, however, should pay for the marriage license and the minister. The bride's dress, accessories, veil, lingerie, and honeymoon clothes are the responsibility of her family, while the groom's family pays for his tuxedo. Everyone else should pay for their own outfits, including groomsmen and bridesmaids. Flowers in the church and also reception, as well as the bridesmaids' flowers, are down to the bride. The groom should cover the bride's bouquet and all corsages for the bride, mothers, and grandmothers. He will also look after the buttonholes for the men of the party.

The groom's family pays for the honeymoon in its entirety, while the bride's family will take care of any photography or videos done at the wedding. Pre-wedding parties are split. The bride will look after the bridesmaids' luncheon, the bridal shower, the hen or bachelorette party, and the engagement party. The groom should take care of the rehearsal dinner, any subsequent engagement parties, and the bachelors' dinner and party. If additional parties or showers are required, these should be taken care of by friends.

The bride should take care of all matters concerning the reception, as well as invitations, announcements and other stationary requirements. The rings are taken care of separately: the bride's family pays for the groom, and vice versa. This is a nice romantic gesture reflecting the joining of the two families. As for transportation, if it is needed between the ceremony and the reception, then the bride and her family should pay it for it.

Note that all of this is just the traditional way things are normally done. That does not mean that every single culture or type of wedding will be the same. In many cases, it may be that things are done differently. If you decide to take care of something yourselves, like the catering or so forth, then the matter of cost will be very different. It may also depend on where the money lies. If one family is far better off than the other, they may decide to take on far more of the costs than usual. On the other hand, it may be that one of the couple does not have a family to support them.

When to Spend and When to Save

There are times when you will need to save up your budget and avoid splashing the cash too much. On the other hand, there will certainly also be times when it is time to spend, without delaying. Knowing the difference can make or break a wedding plan. Most people end up going over their budget by as much as five percent, but if you want to stick to it as much as possible, here are some tips on how to make it work. Although it may sound like a cheat, the first thing to do is actually to increase your budget. This can absolutely be achieved.

As soon as you get engaged, you should start thinking about saving up as much as possible. Even if you are dreaming of a lavish engagement party, it might be time to tighten those belts already and start toning it down. Ultimately, the less money you spend on other things, the more you will have available to spend on your wedding. It is as simple as that! Think about things that you can cut back on at home to save more money for your budget. You should aim to get twenty percent of your earnings stashed away every month – it may take some effort, but it will really help to get that extra cash for the wedding.

You can start by reducing the amount that you spend on certain things. Instead of going out for a drink, buy a bottle of wine and drink at home. Instead of going to the cinema, rent a movie or watch it online. Cut down on the amount of times that you buy food or drink outside of the supermarket, and stock up on the deals instead of going for the things you usually buy. This will have an impact very quickly. You could also cancel any unnecessary subscriptions, and think about cutting back on luxuries. This will help you to get that goal much quicker than you may think, and your quality of life will not drop very far.

Think also about where you save your money. If you can open a new account which has a higher interest rates so much the better. If you have to keep the money in there for a certain amount of time before you can touch it, then that is fine. All you need is to make sure that you have it in time to start booking the big, important costs. You may be surprised at how much interest you can earn. If your families have money set aside, you can ask them to add it to this account if appropriate. Then you can get that interest rate higher. Even if it only earns you pocket change that is still extra money just in case some things cost more than you expected. When the deadlines in your plan start looming, it's time to look for bargains. When you see one, it's okay to spend moderately.

Bargain Tips: How to Save

There are plenty of ways to save money when it comes to actually buying things. The first thing that you will want to do is to look for a credit card or spending system that will earn you points and rewards. Typically, shopping online can be done through a parent service that earns you points. Many cards can add up to things like airline miles or cash back when you spend with them. Look for these and then make sure that you use those systems to pay for absolutely everything. It could add up to some great rewards.

You should also consider decreasing the number of people invited or in your wedding party if you need to save cash.

Demoting someone from bridesmaid to guest will save money on hair, makeup, and gifts. If you struggle to cut the list of guests, then there are some easy things to think about. Children under 12 might not be allowed to stay up long enough to watch the cake cutting or attend the party, so if they wouldn't be allowed, cut them out. If friends want to bring significant others, only allow those in serious relationships. If they are not living together or have not dated for more than a couple of years, they don't have to come.

Be sure to read through any contract that you sign, as well. It may be that vendors add in extra little frills and details that you do not really need. Think about whether anyone will notice the difference if you do not include them in your day. Even if you only save a small amount of money with these cuts, they can add up to big savings overall. Something like only using one color of ink on your invitations instead of two colors can make a world of difference. These little costs are the ones that add up without our realizing it.

You can also save on your wedding photos if you take out unnecessary effects. Sepia toning or focusing on one color in a black and white image just is not cool any more, and the photos normally look clichéd and awful. If you are being charged for special effects like these, just take them out. There is no need for multiple exposures on your wedding day. You just want nicely framed, nicely taken images – the special effects are for fashion photo shoots.

Consider cutting costs by saving the very best things only for the biggest moments. For example, you could go for expensive champagne when it comes time to do the toasts. For the rest of the night, a cheaper brand will do. Most likely, no one will know the difference, especially as they will not be able to see the bottle. You should also always look out for deals and voucher codes. For example, some photographers might offer money off for referrals or those who subscribe to their newsletter. This can really help.

ENGAGEMENT

What Is The Real Purpose of Engagement?

Getting married is one of the greatest events in a person's life. It's the symbol of love, the base of family and the celebration of people and families having met and wanting to live together.

It all starts with the moment in which, with a knee to the floor (most of the time, at least), the man asks the woman to marry him, to make him the happiest man alive.

An engagement is basically a promise to wed and it is also a way of referring to the period of time between the marriage proposal and the marriage itself occurring. During this time, the couple is said to be "affianced," which means that those two persons have the intention of eventually getting married and are somehow letting the world know that they plan to seal their love in holy matrimony.

It's not predetermined how long people are supposed to be engaged for, and it largely varies according to the different cultures and religions of the parties involved. Long engagements were common a long time ago, when couples were determined sometimes even at the moment of birth (by their parents, of course), so they had to wait for many years until they were old enough to wed.

We are used to thinking of the engagement as a period following getting (or giving) an engagement ring and preceding the wedding. Many of us believe that the purpose of engagement is preparation for a wedding. While it is undoubtedly so, this stage in your relationship has a much more important purpose. Let's stop and think about the true meaning of engagement.

Some history

The custom is believed to have started from the Jewish tradition, which was later adopted by the ancient Greeks. The latter made the engagement ring popular for the centuries and up to nowadays. The Greeks used to give the ring to express the deepest form of affection and the sweetest feelings towards their beloved. Once accepted, the ring served to mark the bond between the two people.

In Western culture, the engagement tradition has been observed since the Middle Ages. It was accompanied by placing a ring on the second last finger of the woman's left hand; this had a meaning — people believed back then that the very finger contains "the vein of love", which made the ring closest to her heart. Later in the 16th century, the Italians started to buy diamond rings, which ultimately became a symbol for an everlasting and unbreakable love.

In present-day tradition, although the engagement ring itself is not necessary, wearing it means that the woman's feelings are engaged by a particular man, her betrothed. While the ring is optional, the meaning of engagement should not be neglected. It is a very important transition period from the status of "single" or "in a relationship" to the status of "married".

When the proposal is made and accepted, things get serious. There is nothing to fear though — if the two of you are serious about each other, then you will use this "buffer zone" to communicate, and to clear some blind spots which may be left somewhere, and make plans for the future. Of course, the wedding ceremony should not be left without attention and proper preparation, as you never get to know a person better than while working on a mutual project. Still, the ceremony is not the most important thing.

Things you should know before getting engaged

There's a huge difference between liking, wanting and loving someone. So you should get things straight before taking this big step; not only your and your fiancée's lives are on the table, but also the expectations of lots of family members.

Other things that should be discussed or at least talked about before the proposal are career goals, for example, or whether or not you both want to have kids; in short, the kind of life you are dreaming about leading, because it can be really painful when you come to realize that you want different things after you get married.

It's important that families get to know each other and hopefully get along. When two people get together it's actually more than two people getting together: its two families! So make sure that they all know each other, and that they get to spend some quality time with each other.

Defining the mutual grounds

It is crucial to define the real intentions and expectations of both parties during the engagement in order to have a mutual understanding of each other's roles and responsibilities in the future marriage. This is the right time to talk about your secrets and concerns without the fear of being misunderstood. During the engagement the two of you should learn to envision one another as a spouse and partner in the majority of areas, not just in relation to household issues. You will need to reach an agreement on many important matters: children, place of living, mutual duties and responsibilities, and others. You should not forget to talk about the personal freedom — while every human being has his or her own understanding of such freedom, it is important to feel it in the marriage and not to deprive your significant other of it.

Once the T's are crossed and the I's are dotted, you should make a decision whether or not you are right for each other. It might happen that the engagement period shows incompatibility between the bride and the groom. On the bright side, it's always better to stop the relationship earlier than spend the years with someone who's becoming more and more distant to you. Still, most people move from engagement to the next step, marriage. Mainly because the original purpose of engagement is to allow time for contemplation, the transition to the following stage usually goes nice and smoothly.

Should I drop a knee? Should I hire an airplane with a banner?

There are as many ways to get engaged as people who have gotten engaged in the history of mankind, but there are also a few basic tips that should be considered.

There are people who like to do it in front of the whole world, while others like to keep it private and intimate, just the two of them in a romantic moment that will live in their memories forever.

You may even consider having a small prior chat with her father or maybe an older brother, if the girl (or her family) is a traditional one. In any case, this is going to be one of the most important and definitive moments and decisions of your life, so take a deep look into your heart, think about what she'd love it to be like, and don't feel like you should do it like anybody else did it. Go for your feelings.

Surprises usually work fine. Picking the right spot (maybe one that played an important role in your history) is important, but it is more important that you have picked a beautiful ring. Most girls love rings and of course they love diamonds, but they are also aware that they are really expensive, so don't feel pressure to be extravagant.

Don't forget the magic words, said while looking right into her eyes and down into her soul: will you marry me?

The Rules of Engagement

Engagement is a serious step in every couple's relationship. It is a transition from the dating status to the status of a married couple. The phase bears a very important meaning, as it allows the bride and groom to think about the seriousness of their intentions towards each other, to assess the risks, challenges, and opportunities related to the mutual living as a family, and, of course, to prepare for the wedding.

Engagement can be a lot of fun, as well as being something more like meditation. While it always up to the couple to decide how to spend this magical time, there are some basic rules that it's better to follow. Below are some basic guidelines you may need to consider when you are coming close to the stage of engagement with your loved one.

The proposal

The first thing that will come along is the proposal itself. There is a traditional way of doing this, which involves standing on one knee and having an engagement ring. According to the existing custom, the proposal should be a surprise. The best way for a man to ask his beloved woman to marry him is by doing it in front of witnesses. The act may take place at a party, in a company of friends, or at a dinner with parents. This way, the fiancé underlines the seriousness of his intentions. Besides, it is always nice to share joy with people around you.

The engagement ring

The ring itself has a symbolic meaning. It is a bond that joins two people and represents their emotional connection. It is not a strict rule the couple has to follow, but a tradition that the fiancé would rather consider. Some believe that the ring should cost a small fortune, something between one and three months' salaries. This, however, is not required at all. There is no rule on this matter, but to follow one's own heart (and also to remember about the bride's-to-be preferences regarding jewelry).

The family

Here is an important rule: never forget the family. The people who brought you up, the ones who have been with you during the initial stages of your lives deserve to know the news the earliest. Inform the parents first, and then make an announcement to the rest of the family and close friends.

The planning

Engagement is always about planning for the next step — the wedding. It is about plans for the celebration and also about mutual plans for the future. It is best when the two of you make a schedule of your preparations and divide the responsibilities. It is important to leave enough time to contemplate on the life as a couple that is waiting around the corner.

Duration

There is no particular rule regarding the length of the engagement period. It can last a few months or a year and a half. It all depends on the time they need to think the whole marriage thing through and their readiness to take the next step. What you need to remember is that there is no rush. It's always better to take it slow and then live a happy marriage — after having thrown a splendid and well-prepared wedding.

Engagement Party

An engagement is a great reason for a celebration. All in all, the two people have made a decision to spend their lives together. This is not the beginning of the day-to-day living as a married couple (even though many couples start living together long before the engagement), it is too early for that — so why not give a chance to the lightheartedness and share the good mood with people who are close? Besides, it is a good opportunity for people who are not yet acquainted to get to know each other.

Who organizes it?

Earlier in history, the father of the bride used to host a party at which the engagement was announced. Back then, it was a complete surprise to the guests who, after hearing the news, expressed their true emotions and who could not bring gifts, as they had known nothing of the engagement. Currently, the tradition that dictates that the bride's parents organize the party has partially remained. The majority of modern-day couples, however, leaves the arrangement to them or trusts the party planning to their friends.

Surely, when delegating the organization of the engagement party to someone else, you will have to think of the expenses. While it used to be customary for the bride's side of the family to pay the bill some time ago, it is now usually up to the spouses-to-be. Of course, when one of your friends agrees to back you up, you must acknowledge that it's you who will cover the costs.

Who comes to a party?

The interesting — and probably the most worrisome — part of the engagement party is whom to invite. Consider sending invitations to those whom you want to see at your wedding. Of course, if you want to announce the news (and celebrate it) to an even a greater number of people, you can even make several parties instead of just one — a light one for colleagues, a casual one for your buddies (or your ladies' club), etc. What you have to remember is that you should never forget the parents and your close families, and also you don't have to make a celebration for every single person you know — better think of whom you want to share some joy with and go with them.

The theme & your appearance

The whole concept of the engagement party should be a challenging thing to come up with. You should probably pick a theme that speaks a lot about the two of you or one that you are comfortable with. It can be a beach party, or a backyard BBQ, or even a celebration in a small hotel (but make sure to book the entire thing beforehand) — it just should not be fancier than the wedding. The same goes for the clothes you are going to wear. On the one hand, it's not as a casual event to look as you usually do, but it's not the official big ceremony yet. Keep it simple and stylish, and also review your budget frequently.

The engagement party is held when the couple is celebrating their engagement to one another. The scale, theme, and the guest list strictly depend on your budget and your preferences regarding the people present. Keep it slightly simpler than the wedding and remember that you have more planning to do soon — don't get taken away by celebrations; rather, spare yourself time to concentrate on the important things between you and your betrothed.

Engagement rings

Of course, you will want to prepare just the right proposal when asking that special someone to marry you, but you also need to find the perfect engagement ring to offer during the proposal. Some couples shop for the engagement ring together, but let's be honest; she wants you to know her well enough to do it on your own and get it right. It is always more romantic to surprise her with the perfect ring.

In western countries and civilizations, women more than men commonly wear engagement rings; although there are certain cultures and countries in which they are worn both by women and men.

Engagement rings, also called promise rings, usually feature gemstones and/or a diamond (ideally). Men usually present them to women, when their intentions of getting married are explicit, and the ring has great romantic significance since it means before society that the man and the woman want everybody to know that they love each other and will get married, in time.

The story of the diamond on the ring

Diamond rings became tradition when Archduke Maximilian of Austria proposed to Mary of Burgundy, in 1477, with a ring that held thin, flat diamonds in the form of an "M". Apparently, that was the first spark that started the fire among European aristocracy and nobility. We've come a long way, and we're still honoring the Archduke's gesture to his Mary.

Diamonds are the strongest rocks in the world, and because of their strength and beauty they signify enduring love between lovers.

Also, the fact that they are so expensive and hard to get (especially until the discovery of the African diamond mines in the 1870's) adds significance and meaning to the strength of the bond and the love behind it; you don't just buy diamonds for any girl.

From a fashion point of view, diamonds are as versatile and classy as jewelry gets and can be worn with practically any outfit on any occasion: with jeans at a party, with a dress for cocktails or, of course, with a wedding gown in a wedding. Still, choosing the right diamond ring is quite a task, one that grooms face with more than a few doubts and a great deal of hesitation.

After all, according to the De Beer Company's classic slogan: "A diamond is forever."

How to buy an engagement ring

Before you stroll into the first jewelry store, you need to go on a couple of serious reconnaissance missions. First, figure out the size. Sneak the ring your girlfriend wears on her other ring finger and trace the inside size on a piece of paper. The jeweler will be able to figure the correct size from your tracing. Second, call in the spies. Your girlfriend's girlfriends know what she likes. They have talked and window-shopped this prized possession for years. Be sure you choose the friend that will keep the secret though, don't choose the blabbermouth.

One last step before you begin shopping. Set your budget. We have all the absurd idea that you're supposed to spend the equivalent to three month's salary when buying an engagement ring. Don't believe the hype. As impressive as a sparkling, oversized diamond ring may be, marrying a man who is fiscally responsible is a much better investment. Be reasonable in your expenditures, but not cheap. Cheap is never good. Look at what you make in an average month to six weeks and use that as the starting point for you budget.

Once the shopping begins, you're looking for the 4C's:

- *Clarity* is the reference point for fractures in the rock. You're looking at the level of imperfections or inclusions. On a scale of F (for flawless) to I3 (the most inclusions), your best bet for the budget is usually in the SI1-SI2 range. This diamond isn't perfect but it will sparkle impressively.
- *Color* isn't actually about color. It's more about the absence of color. White diamonds range from colorless to yellow. Color is measured in tiers with D, E, and F being the clearest, whitest diamonds. G, H, It is the second tier and a good choice for most rings. If you get all the way to Z, you'll have a yellow diamond.

- *Cut* is the way the diamond is cut or graded to reflect light. This is where the shape of the diamond comes into play and the information provided by the friend.

  Shapes include:
  - Round – It's a circle.
  - Marquis – An oval shape with pointy ends.
  - Emerald – Rectangle with beveled, rounded edges
  - Princess – Square with a flat-top and specific cut design along the edges.
  - Pear – Teardrop shape
  - Asscher – Square base without pointed edges, flat face with parallel lines around the sides.
  - Heart – It's a heart.
  - Cushion – Square or rectangle with rounded edges and flat facets.

  - *Carat* is the weight of the diamond. The average engagement ring is right around one carat. Carats greatly affect budget. Opting for something just under the full carat mark will save you money. So instead of choosing the two carat ring, look for a 1.9 instead.

She said yes! Now what?

Now it's wedding planning time! There are lots of things to do, like picking the perfect place, deciding on the music, making guest lists, choosing a menu, and so on; this is just another stage in the happiest period of your life.

WEDDING PLANNING TIMELINE AND CHECKLIST

Importance of Planning and Scheduling

A marriage ceremony is generally comprised of many events and it varies between cultures, religion and ethnicity. Nevertheless, numerous common features are notably visible including mutual visit, sending gifts and well wishing, exchanging of different customary dresses, ornaments, cosmetics and so on. For a successful marriage to happen, planning and scheduling of many events are critically important keeping in mind that any mismanagement or misunderstanding can damage the reputation of any parties involved in the process.

What are Planning and Scheduling of a Wedding Ceremony

Planning and scheduling a wedding is of great importance in executing a happy and successful marriage ceremony. In essence, planning and scheduling are intertwined and interconnected. Planning a wedding involves the overall process of wedding and writes it down in some distinguished chronological events. On the other hand, scheduling occurs when the tasks of a wedding are coherently and succinctly distributed among various personnel on a day-to-day basis in a way that leads up to a successful wedding.

Cost Minimization

A wedding is undoubtedly one of the most expensive events in our life. In most cases, actual cost exceeds the anticipated cost by a great margin. When we think of minimizing cost without reducing the glamour and uniqueness of a wedding, planning and scheduling are the most effective options. For example, if you can plan well to whom you are inviting, you will be able to avoid the unnecessary cost of rampant inviting and other associated costs. You will be able to narrow down your target inviting guests. It is worth mentioning that you are supposed to invite those who significantly matter in your life.

Distribution of Tasks and Successful Coordination

A wedding entails a lot of tasks to be done. From inviting relatives to managing community center, there is a huge amount of work to be done. Planning and scheduling helps you distribute tasks among the volunteers and personnel, and to carefully control and monitor the whole process. Moreover, it helps keep track of progress of many simultaneous functions of wedding and adjust accordingly if and when necessary. You can easily grasp the process without going much into every event.

Satisfaction of Making a Wedding Successful

When you start planning a wedding ceremony or something similar, you need to make sure that everyone is quite happy, since any discontent from anybody involved in the process can have a gloomy impact on wedding ceremony and beyond. Here comes planning and scheduling to the fore as you can estimate the capacity of workload on can undertake and efficiently accomplish. Without planning, you risk sliding into a chaotic environment making a wedding ceremony nothing short of a nightmare, which could haunt you for years.

Like most of the events of our life, planning and scheduling are a must in accomplishing a successful and memorable wedding ceremony. Do not put your point of happiness to chance.

Six Months To One Year Before

Now that the romantic proposal is behind you, it's time to start planning for your future. As you begin thumbing through bridal magazines and dreaming of the wedding day, you may find that some dreams from your childhood are still relevant today. When you put those lifelong desires together with newly formed wishes, the result can be a lovely ceremony with your very personality stamped upon it.

One year before the date, the very first action should be to make a list of everything you want to include in the wedding. This should encompass a budget, wedding date and time, number of bridesmaids and groomsmen, preferred colors, favored venues for the ceremony and reception, and initial guest list, or at least an estimated number of guests expected.

Don't worry; you can change your mind about any of these items as time goes on. Right now, an outline will simply give you direction and peace of mind as you wade into the abyss of wedding planning details.

Let the shopping begin! Now is the time to hit those bridal shops and try on every gown that catches your fancy. Set a price before you go shopping and stay within your budget, but let your inner princess shine. This is the one day you will be the most beautiful woman in the room. Choose a wedding dress that makes you feel lovely. There's no right or wrong here. Your vision is the only one that matters.

About eight months before the wedding you should have the gown purchased so you'll have plenty of time for fittings. Narrow down your choices for flowers and other décor, music, food and drinks for the reception, and style and flavor of the wedding cake.

This is also the perfect time to visit a few stores and register for gifts. If you have family and friends coming in from out of town, be sure to choose at least one store that has either nationwide locations or online shopping available. One great option is placing a registry on Amazon. Simply go to Amazon Wedding and choose Wedding Registry from the drop down menu.

Reserve an appropriate number of rooms at a nearby hotel for guests who will need to spend the night. Many will give price breaks for wedding guests. Check with your local hotels and research the price as well as number of guests required to receive a discount.

It's time to take action and book all the details you have been planning around six months prior to the wedding date. Order the bridesmaids gowns, the wedding cake, and book your musical choice and caterer. Discuss honeymoon plans with your fiancée and choose a trip that suits you both.

You're getting busier now, and it will not ease up until the wedding is over. Take a deep breath, and try to relax. Allow your excitement to overflow and make planning fun. The joy is in the details, and if you let love be your number one priority, your wedding day will be the fairy tale of your dreams.

Three To Four Months Before

Most young girls dream of the perfect wedding day. A glorious time filled with sunshine, love, and promises, where an ordinary person is transformed into a princess for one magical day.

Planning a wedding is one of the most exciting times in a woman's life. It can become quite stressful, however, to live up to the dreams from your childhood. If there is no organization and many details are left for the last minute, the beautiful, anticipated wedding could turn into a nightmare.

Don't fear, we have the solution to make sure your timeline runs smoothly and the stress is kept to a minimum. Remember to take joy in the details, involve your family and friends, and wedding planning can become something quite magnificent and fun.

Three to four months before the wedding date, you'll want to start solidifying details such as the following.

Decide on a design for the wedding cake, meet with bakers, and get that lovely confection ordered. There are so many different ways to go with the wedding cake, from sweet to sassy, traditional to fun, and the list goes on. If you find the classic white wedding cake boring, then go with something more interesting, such as red velvet, pink champagne, or coconut lime. Put personal details in the wedding toppers. Find a bride and groom topper that highlights the personalities of yourself and your fiancée.

This is the perfect time to shop for and order invitations. You will be choosing the card design, font, color, envelopes, and more. A lot of thought goes into the invitations, and a custom order such as this takes a while to print, so be sure to get this out of the way fairly early. If you plan on hiring a calligrapher to address the envelopes, get started on that at the three to four month pre-wedding period as well. Double check the guest list to be certain all addresses are up to date.

The rings! Possibly the most important decision, as you will be looking at these every day after the wedding. Should the rings of the bride and groom match? Do you prefer white gold, yellow gold, silver, or titanium? Answer these questions and shop thoroughly to be sure you are happy with your purchase.

The groom should rent the formalwear for men of the wedding party. If choosing alternative transportation such as a horse and carriage or a limousine, these should be reserved at this time.

Make plans for the rehearsal dinner. Finalize the guest list and book the venue. The rehearsal dinner can be as elegant as a formal meal in a five star restaurant, or as casual as a barbecue in the park.

Organization and delegation will keep the wedding preparation timeline running smoothly. Bridesmaids and groomsmen, as well as family and close friends, are usually very happy to help. Let them. Don't let stress overtake the joy. Treasure the excitement, the pleasure, and most especially, the love. Now go forth, and plan that wedding!

Two Months Before

Two months before the wedding is when the reality starts to sink in and the countdown begins. All the plans that have been made so far are coming together. Certainly there have been some bumps in the road, but what doesn't kill us only makes us stronger, right?

The past several months were more than likely spent on shopping, discussing, and ordering various details and materials. Now is the time to take action.

The invitations that have been so lovingly and painstakingly chosen and designed should be ready to place into the mail. It's important to give the guests plenty of time to mark their calendars and save the date for your special day.

Contact the venues and services you have booked to confirm that everything is running on schedule. If the deposits have not yet been paid, this is a good time to take care of that.

Have a meeting with your chosen photographer and discuss all your desires beforehand. It's a good idea to do some photos before the ceremony so the time between wedding and reception is not overly lengthy. Some opportunities beforehand include group photos with the bride and bridesmaids and her family, the groom and groomsmen and family, and shots of the bride alone.

Check with your local newspaper and submit a picture of the happy couple for the wedding announcement.

Consult with whatever type of music you have hired for the reception and go over the playlist. Details such as the father/daughter dance, the first dance as bride and groom, and any other specialties will have certain song choices attached to them. Be sure your instructions have been heeded to circumvent a mistake on the big day.

For those who are writing personal vows, get those thoughts down on paper now so the editing process can begin.

Finalize honeymoon plans. If you will be leaving the country, make sure passports and other identification are up to date. Purchase appropriate honeymoon attire.

Fittings of the wedding gown and bridesmaids' dresses should be well under way by this time. It may take several fittings to acquire the desired fit. It is important to wear the shoes you have chosen for the wedding day during the fitting so the dress will fall to the correct length. Purchase undergarments for the wedding day, paying special attention to the type of gown you will be wearing, and wear these to the fitting as well.

Buy wedding accessories such as bride and groom wine glasses, a guest book, cake knife, gifts for bridesmaids and groomsmen, a ring pillow, and any other special details you would like to include.

Take a day with your bridesmaids to visit the beauty shop and decide on the best hairstyles for the wedding. This will not only take the guesswork out of choosing a style on the wedding day, but will also allow for better time management.

By now you should be able to see a glimpse of how glorious your wedding day will be. Congratulations, your wedding day is almost here!

A Month Before the Big Day

Five Quintessential Things To Check Off Your Wedding Plan

With so many essentials that need to be covered and decisions to be made, planning for your wedding seems to be a daunting task. According to successful wedding planners, it usually takes a year to plan a wedding, and within this period you have covered most of the essential tasks that you need to tackle. However, there are certain small details that you still need to deal with as the big day approaches. And while it may not be that much, these smallest things are quintessential to the success of your most special day. Thus, it would be helpful to pay attention to these parts of your wedding checklist.

A month before the big day, you may feel comfortable with the accomplishments you have made in your wedding preparation. But there are tasks in your checklist that remain to be accomplished including follow-ups on the previous wedding preparations that you have already started. Here are the wedding errands that you still need to check off your wedding planning list one month before your wedding day:

Apply for a marriage license

A month before your intended wedding date is the ideal time to apply for your marriage license. You can check with the local bureau or the state where you intend to wed. Most of the local civil registry has online site where you can check the license requirements but it is most advisable to call the clerk's office or inquire in person. After you have accomplished this, do not forget to give a copy of your license to your mom or your maid of honor for safekeeping.

Have the Final Dress Fitting

It is essential to do the final dress fitting a month before your wedding date. This will give your designer ample time to make necessary adjustments, if needed. Be sure to try out also all the accessories to check how they fit the whole ensemble and make any necessary changes as needed. It is also best to bring along your maid of honor during the final fitting so she could learn how to bustle your dress. Ensure also that all the bridesmaids have their gowns ready for the big event.

Make Last Minute Adjustments with Vendors

You may need to talk to your vendors regarding some last minute adjustments on your wedding details. By this time, you need to confirm the floral orders to your florist and arrange for the delivery time. Finalize the details with your photographer and videographer and give them your preferred shot list. Review the music with the DJ or band, finalize your playlist and confirm special request songs. Make the salon appointments for your hair, make-up, manicure and pedicure.

Create your wedding program

Your wedding program is necessary so your guests would know the flow of your wedding event. It should be prepared by this time and ensure that copies are handed out to your guests.

Discuss your Wedding Ceremony with your Officiant

Whether you are going to have a church wedding or a civil one, it is important that you discuss the details of your wedding ceremony to your officiate. It would help him/her know how you want your special day be celebrated.

Final Week Preparation for Your Nuptial Day

One week before your wedding day, most of the couples start to feel the jitters in anticipation of the most important event that will happen to them. Some couple may feel exhausted with all the preparations that they have made and some details may be left unchecked. But if you want to lessen the stress of the wedding preparation, it is important not feel lazy during this final week of your prep time. It is then absolutely necessary to accomplish the following details to put your mind at ease and have a hassle-free nuptial day.

Finalize the Headcount

One of the most important things to do during this final week is to review your RSVPs and confirm the guest headcount to your venue manager and your caterer. Do not forget to include your suppliers such as your photographers, videographers and band members who still need to be included in your meal plan. Specify with your caterer how many extra plates he needs to prepare. You need to inform your venue manager for specific vendor requests such as location of the DJ booth or a set up space needed by the florist.

Finalize the Seating Chart

You will want to be sure that all your guests have a specific place to sit during your wedding. First, it will save up your guests the trouble of guessing where their assigned table is, and second, it will be helpful with the wait staff during the serving of your meal entrees. It will be best to sit friends and acquaintances together whenever possible so none of your guests feel left out during the wedding reception. However, you may also choose to play matchmaker and seat together friends that may have the potential to hit it off. It is also essential to print place and table cards together with the final seating chart.

Confirm Final Arrangements with your Wedding Vendors

Although you have made the final detail confirmations with your vendors one month prior to tying the knot, it is important to confirm the final arrangements with them one week prior to the event. This will clear out all necessary instructions for your suppliers specifically logistics. It is essential to give the ceremony and venue managers the schedule of vendor deliveries and setup times, including the contact details of each suppliers. In this way, logistics details can be efficiently covered.

Confirm Your Honeymoon Travel Arrangements

Whether going out of town or just staying at a hotel within your locale, it is crucial to confirm your honeymoon arrangements a week before the wedding. If you are travelling, you need to finalize all travel arrangements during this period. You may start packing your bags for your honeymoon and get traveler's checks and prepare small amount of foreign cash as needed. Confirm your hotel bookings, as well.

Pick up Wedding Dress

Don't forget to pick up your wedding dress a week before tying the knot. This will give you ample time to check on the final adjustments made by your supplier.

Attend Bachelor/ Bachelorette Party

Generally, there is no definitive time when to throw the bachelor/bachelorette party for would-be groom and bride. However, most preferred to hold it after all the hustle and bustle of the wedding preparation is almost done, i.e., a week before the big date. So, celebrate your last few days of singlehood with your friends, have fun and take this as your time out from all the jitters of your wedding planning.

A Day before Saying "I Do"

It is a day before your big day and you have almost completed checking off the essential things that you must do from your wedding plan checklist. This is the day you started to feel more relaxed. Albeit, with all the tasks accomplished for your wedding preparation, some couples may still feel at lost 24 hours before they finally walk down the aisle. You may have accomplished everything but you may still feel that there are still more work to be done to make sure that you will have a hassle-free, successful wedding day. Here are some ideas on how to handle the last 24 hours before the big day and to minimize the worries on your mind:

Attend the Rehearsal Dinner

The rehearsal dinner is traditionally held the night before the wedding and is a great opportunity for both families to get to know each other before the wedding day in a more laid-back setting. Take advantage of this relaxed environment and enjoy spending some quality time with your families. It also helps you shake off the pre-wedding tension and make everyone feel invited and comfortable with the upcoming nuptials.

Pack your Wedding Essential Kit and Lay out your "Getting Ready" Clothes

Gather together all of your necessary accessories and pack them in one clutch. It is also best to prepare some beauty emergency kits that may come in handy for some unforeseen beauty emergencies. You also need to prepare your "getting ready" clothes for dressing up the following day to you time deciding what you want to wear for that "getting ready" pictorials.

Meet with the Bridesmaids and the Groomsmen

For the bride, it is imperative to meet with the bridesmaids and have one final girls meeting to and go over together the ceremony and to discuss their duties just to make sure that all are of the same mindset. The bride can also hand over to one of her bridesmaids the wedding essential kit and distribute the bridal gifts to all the girls. This is also the applicable with the groom and the groomsmen. It is important to have one final discussion between the groom and his groomsmen and remind everyone of what is expected of them during the wedding day. You may also use this time to have some fun and reminisce of some good memories together.

Call Your Suppliers One Last Time

Just to confirm that everything is going according to schedule, you may call your suppliers one more time within this final 24 hours before the wedding day. This gives you the assurance that problems may not occur during the day itself. This is also the best time to write the checks and/or talk to your suppliers about any final balances to be paid at the end of the reception.

Write a Note for Your Groom

For the bride, the final 24 hours before the wedding day is the best time to write a little love note to your groom and let the best man hand it over to him. This may be sweet and short or sexy and passionate. Either way, this will add up to the excitement of you two meeting in front of the altar come wedding day.

Your Final Moment - Walking Down the Aisle Stress-free

Finally, it is happening! You wake up on your wedding day giddy with excitement and anticipation. After all the months of preparation, you are now ready to walk down the aisle and say goodbye to singlehood. Your wedding day is the most important day for you and your partner, and should be celebrated with fun-filled memories and lots of love. Since you have released all the stress related to your wedding preparation, here are some tips you can do on this momentous day to ensure that your journey to your "happily ever after" will be filled with joy.

Wake Up Refreshed

Yes, you might not be able to sleep because of excitement the night before but it is imperative that you give your body a good night's rest so you will wake up refreshed on your wedding day. Waking up refreshed will help you set your mood for the whole event. After all, no one wants to feel groggy on his/her wedding day.

Eat a Good Breakfast

Having a hearty breakfast will give you the energy boost you need to last through the day of your big event. Be sure that you get a good one. It would help if you will be served with your favorite high protein and complex carbohydrates food since you will be sure to spend most of your wedding day without food.

Give yourself plenty of time to get ready

It is essential that you have plenty of time to get ready before walking down the aisle. This will relieve you from any stress relative to dressing up for your special day. Attend your hairstyle and make up appointment on time. Ask your photographer to come early so they can set up and shoot your wedding preparation time without risking of running out of time. This will give you ample time to relax and have little chit chats with your entourage and not worry about the time that you will be finished.

Present Parents and Each Other With Gifts

The day of your wedding is the best time to thank your parents for all the good things and good memories that they have spent with you from your childhood up to your special day. A better way of showing your gratitude on your wedding day is to present them with gifts. A simple, well-chosen gift for both your mom and dad will make them feel gratified. Also, this is the best time to show your partner how much you appreciate them by handing them a well-deserved, loving gift. This will give them a sense of appreciation and love will make them feel elated and special on your wedding day.

Walk Down the Aisle and Enjoy the Moment

Your wedding day is your path to your togetherness. It is important that you walk down the aisle with much happiness more than anything else. So when the time comes to tie the knot, smile, enjoy the moment and let your love for each other make your wedding day special.

THE WEDDING CEREMONY

The Happiest Day

Your wedding day will be the happiest day of your life and you have been dreaming about it since you were a little girl. Therefore, it is important that all of the moving pieces of the wedding come together without a hitch – and there are a lot of moving pieces. Once you get engaged, the whirlwind process of selecting a dress and tux, finding the wedding hall of your dreams, finding the right caterer and band begins – and it won't stop until you say "I do". That's why we are going to give you some tips and ideas about how to actively create the wedding of your dreams.

First, you will need to decide on a wedding style or theme. Will you have an outdoor wedding, will the wedding be in a church or perhaps you would like a destination wedding. Once you have decided the type of wedding you would like, you can then start looking for the right venue. Keep in mind that not every beautiful hall is the right one – this is because the venue needs to be big enough to fit all of your guests comfortably. Once you have found the right hall, your next step will be to determine who will be officiating the wedding – make sure to book him/her well in advance. Choosing an officiant can be a difficult process, especially for inter-faith marriages. This is a topic that you and your betrothed should speak about early on. If you are planning on having a religious officiant, whose religion will he/she represent? Perhaps you will have two officiants, one representing each religion. If this is the case, you need to determine if both officiants are comfortable with this arrangement. At the end of the day you two are getting married because you love each other – so make sure you find an officiant who understands that and makes it their priority.

Once you have secured the hall, have a theme in mind and having settled on the right officiant, then the time has come to start focusing on the details. First, begin thinking about rings. Saving for the right ring can take some time and cost a pretty penny. Additionally, if you are having a ring designed you may need to give the jeweler several months' notice. Next, you need to consider who the bridesmaids and groomsmen will be. A good way to approach this topic is to first select how many of both you want. Then you can more easily make your selection from close friends and family. Now that you are well on your way and the wedding day is getting closer, you need to decide on a photographer and videographer. Keep in mind that you do not want to wait until the last minute – good photographers can be booked months in advance.

As the planning stage of the wedding moves along, you will need to work out a few more details. Who will be hosting the rehearsal dinner and where? What kind of flowers and decoration do you want? Who will be in charge of securing your marriage license and which band will be serenading you and your one true love during your first dance? For all of these issue and more, we have the guidance you need.

Wedding Styles and Themes

With so many wedding themes and styles to choose from, who knows where to begin? For every general theme, there can be hundreds of different styles you can incorporate. Therefore, when determining the theme and style of your wedding you need to take a focused approach. First, you need to determine your likes and dislikes as a couple. Are you the type of people who want a formal black tie wedding – or are you more laid back? If you are more laid back, how much more? There is a big difference between a formal wedding and barefoot wedding on the beach. Once you have determined how formal or informal you want your wedding to be, it's time to do some introspection. What type of wedding will best match your personalities, both as individuals and as a couple? This is what will allow you to feel the most comfortable at your wedding and will grant you maximum enjoyment. This is where themes become important.

There are almost an infinite number of themes and combinations of various styles that you can create for your wedding. We are going to explore just a handful to help better acquaint you with some of your options.

The Classic Wedding

The "Classic Wedding" takes many forms. However, many traditionalists prefer to have the ceremony in a church or another place of worship. Usually the music choices are very traditional including the Wedding March and Canon in D. Frequently this type of wedding utilizes white and blush color schemes. The ceremony is performed by a religious officiant (though not always) and the wedding party is typically wearing coordinated dress. Due to the lack of space in most places of worship, the reception is often held at a different venue. Decorations at the reception hall often are similar to those at the ceremony and follow a similar color scheme.

The Vineyard Wedding

Though slightly more laid back, the vineyard wedding offers both the beauty of the outdoors and the elegance of the vineyard itself. Typically, vineyard weddings will host the ceremony on the side of the vineyard – often overlooking hills flowing with grape vines. Due to the outdoor nature of the wedding, the couple has much more leeway in dress code. Because vineyards are typically more elegant, black tie fits well. However, being in the outdoors also allows for a more relaxed dress code. Often at vineyard weddings the vineyard will set up a large tent to host your guests for dinner/ or lunch and will provide a nice dance floor and place for the band. The color scheme for the reception is very open – as the back drop of the vineyard is what really creates the ambiance.

The Beach Wedding

The beach wedding is perfect for lovers of the ocean. Typically the beach wedding is very laid back, both in dress and in ceremony. Many couples who opt for the beach wedding have smaller guest lists – as the ceremony is generally standing room only. A popular option is to have the ceremony as the sun sets over the water, creating a backdrop of beautiful reds and oranges. Normally, the reception will be held at a separate location and varies from couple to couple.

Making Vows that Change You

Writing your vows can be scary for multiple reasons. First and foremost, when you recite your vows, you will most likely be expressing your innermost emotions in front of a couple hundred of your closest family and friends. Moreover, your vows are meant to be something that you stick to – a vow by definition is a pledge to act or behave in a particular manner. So creating the right vows, vows that are both meaningful and life changing, is no small task. Here are a few tips that will help you in writing meaningful, life changing vows.

First, you are getting married because you found your one true love. Love is a precious, rare thing to find. Take several hours to think deeply about your betrothed. What is it about that person that you love so much? What is it about that person that makes you want to spend the rest of your life with him/her? Once you answer these questions, you are on your way.

Next, know your audience and know your comfort level. While it is a wonderful thing for someone to pour their heart and soul out – if this is something you are not comfortable with it can provoke a lot of anxiety. Therefore, if you are a more reserved person, think about things that you have done with your fiancé, things you have seen or spoken about. Things that you know only the two of you will recognize. By mentioning emotions through shared experiences you are able to maintain a certain level of privacy – while at the same time making the most profound gesture to your loved one.

Next, come up with a few or several promises – they are called vows after all. When thinking of your actual vows, i.e.

the promises, try to avoid clichés. If your goal is to make vows that can change your life and your marriage – try to keep them realistic and relevant to your relationship. Though it is advisable to insert a few generic vows, such as "I promise to always love you" or "I promise to always support you," you can personalize them by adding to them. For example, "I promise to always say I love you every night before bed" or "I promise to always support you – through thick and thin, happiness and sadness." Lastly, add vows that are personal to the two of you. Something that you are able to come up with based on your shared experiences together.

Finally, make sure to practice saying your vows out loud. It can be scary confessing your true love and vowing yourself to your betrothed in front of hundreds of people. So make sure to practice. Our advice is that you write out your vows very clearly and practice saying them in front of the mirror – yes, the mirror. It may sound silly, but looking yourself in the eye while practicing your vows will both make you more confident and will let you feel the love your fiancé will be receiving from you at that moment. Remember, practice makes perfect.

Issue of Faith

Faith is the single most important thing in any relationship without which marital life can turn out to be a disaster and in any many cases, relationships have been seen to fail to reach marriage due to the lack of trust between the couples. We live in a world of superfast communication technology in which it is very difficult to cover up what you are doing, which is detrimental to your relationship. We are exposed to a great number of social media enabling us to engage with different relationships simultaneously resulting in an exponential increase in divorce rates. It is not at all surprising that many marriages end within a few days to a few weeks of the wedding.

When you are betrothed to someone to marry within a year or a month or even a week, the issue of faith is of paramount importance involving multiple considerations and moral judgment. The person you are going to marry has been on tight schedules for months and is weaving a lot of dreams around you for an indefinite future to come. There are ways you can deepen trust before the wedding ceremony.

1. Do not Be close to anyone else

You cannot possibly tell who is going to win your heart anytime soon. The human mind works in a very subtle and uncertain way. That does not necessarily justify that you can cheat on someone to whom you are betrothed. The best way to keep yourself faithful and trustworthy is to maintain a substantial distance with your colleagues, co-workers, and your office mates etc.

2. Face-to-communications

Do not throw your relationships away to virtual apparatus like email, Facebook, Viber, Whatsup, etc., knowing that face-to-face contact has no equal when it comes to relationships. A relationship is cemented through continuous shared moments and times. It fosters a greater sense of mutual dependency as you become vulnerable to each other. Passing some moments in a park or a recreational spot bears more significance than exchanging thousands of text messages and emoticons online.

3. Do not impose, rather accommodate

No two people on Earth can think or do alike. When you forget this, you drag your relationship to a thorny space filled with hatred and mutual distrust. There will happen to be a lot of mutual differences with your partner. Do not ever attempt to make changes through an authoritative role, rather acknowledge them with an open mind. You have to accommodate many things that you do not take for granted. Respect what your partner likes or loves to do. In the course of time, she will feel you from her heart and appreciate you, making a heavenly family life you have always dreamt of.

4. Apologize- it won't lower your dignity

Nobody is above error. Whenever you make a mistake, do not wait. Admit your wrongdoing. Otherwise, you risk giving space to misunderstandings arising. You may fear losing your self-esteem when making an apology. Do not forget that making an apology makes you humble- a quality instrumental to a long term relationship.

5. Balance you work vs. family life

It is your family life that comes first in any situation. Never give priority to your work over family life. It will lead to long term painful conditions in life.

Faith is like a fragile glass. Preserve it with utmost sincerity. Hope your wedding day will be the best day of your life.

Finding an Officiant

Your wedding day is truly a very big day as you want to remember every detail of that day to the last moment of life. You are the center of everything and you want to smile with all the others attending your wedding. For the most part of the pre-wedding days, you have been extremely busy in doing never ending tasks leading to the wedding day. However, you may be prone to forgetting one important task: to find the right wedding officiant that suits you and your partner. Your wedding officiant has a lot to do make your big day a memorable one or turn it into a painful memory. There are ways you can find a suitable officiant for your wedding day. To find the right officiant for your wedding ceremony the first thing you need to figure out is what you expect from the officiant in the first place. You might have different choices on what kind of marriage you prefer. You might aspire for a secular ceremony while your father insists on a traditional ceremony with the color of religion. You might end up disliking the performance of the officiant who is extremely methodical or carefree. Here are some of the most important tips which will help you to find the right officiant for the ceremony.

Find Someone You are Comfortable With

On the wedding day, you find yourself significantly tense as you are in the midpoint of a transition in your life. A mixed feeling of joy and fear besets you on all sides. So seek an officiant who has the sensitivity for such a ceremony and who can sympathize with you. This is why you should meet the officiant in person at least once before the wedding day. Share some of your personal feelings regarding the wedding day so that the officiant can equip himself with the necessary preparations to make you feel comfortable and easygoing.

Your Faith Matters

Your family and relatives have a defined orientation to a particular faith or spiritual guidelines. Even in your religion, there are numerous denominations with differing religious, social and cultural worldviews. Before finding an officiant, do not forget to make sure that he is from your own denomination or faith origin if you want to maintain a high level of coherency and consistency in the ceremonial ambience on the wedding day.

A Customized Officiant in a World of Mass Customization

We live in a world of high specialization and division of labor. Parallel to material goods and products, there are noticeable customizations in the service sector including wedding ceremonies. To cater for modern couples, there are many officiants who are highly trained to serve on the basis of likings, choices, customs, rituals, faiths, etc. Many are open minded and readily work with your family members or friends in doing a ceremony for marriage couples from all types of backgrounds.

Interfaith Marriage- Be Clear and Honest

Issues may arise when you are settling into an interfaith marriage, so be clear and straightforward in choosing an officiant. This is not surprising that many officiants would instantly leave the ceremony after discovering an interfaith marriage. For example a Muslim officiant is likely to refuse to serve in such cases. So find someone who doesn't have such issues and is willing to cooperate with you in the sacrament of marriage.

So the bottom line is that you should work out on what kind of ceremony you want and then find the right officiant based on that choice. Hopefully your marriage will then go on smoothly and fine.

Constructing Your Wedding Ceremony

The wedding ceremony is a special day for you and your fiancé. Probably you have waited so long to be pronounced husband and wife for an indefinite time in the future. That is why the wedding day deserves super special attention as a glowing spotlight for a relationship. You can add special flavor to your wedding ceremony by personalizing the ceremony with your own articulated design and plan. If properly planned and implemented, you can make a truly big day worth remembering for your entire lifetime.

From writing marital vows, to center stage designing, to the final sacrament of a wedding, you can craft your likings and choices. This is how you can do it.

Creative Touches in the Events

You can easily differentiate your ceremony by adding some creative touches for the events of the day. The procession can be a major source of creative display. You and your fiancé can walk down from stages set in two different sides of a garden or a park to a mid-point where you will meet. Or you can walk around a circular path with floral decoration to meet at some spot. You can choreograph the music or band party in a way that represents your family traditions.

Intimate Seating Arrangements

Unlike the traditional separated seating placements of bride and groom sides, you can arrange the seating in circular settings so that the guests can see each other, with the bride and the groom seated in the middle. You can request the guests to join hands and surround you in a circle while exchanging your marital vows.

Wedding Readings - Elicit Your Poet from Within

The wedding reading is a once in a lifetime chance to express who you are in the inside. Do not make it faltering filler or hurried mumbling. Many guests will remember your readings after forgetting you. Let the readings be an introduction to your personality, to your partner and to people around the ceremony. Take the necessary time to prepare your readings and make amendments until it is truly articulate and sweet sounding.

Let Your Guests Be Part of Your Ceremony

Despite being extremely busy before the awaited day, do not forget to stay in contact with the people you value the most in your life and vice versa. Let them feel that they are important people in your life. Exchange greetings with each of them and tell them that you will be very happy to see their presence at your wedding. Otherwise they may feel left behind in your moments of enjoyment.

Let Something Grow alongside Your Marital Life

There are some simple things in life that have minimal cost but the emotional effects of those things are truly transcendent. What about planting a tree on the wedding day? It will grow ever after evoking the memory of your wedding in each passing wedding anniversary. The planting site should be prepared the day before the wedding with two containers filled with soil. After putting the plant into the hole, the bride and groom will fill the hole with soil from the container. The tree, in time, can be a source of happy moments and inspiration.

You can personalize your whole wedding day according to your likings. But do not forget to discuss the plan with your partner. You together with your partner can begin a brand new conjugal life based on mutual respect and cooperation from the very wedding ceremony. We hope that divine blessings will be your company on the wedding day!

Wedding Rings

Modern society has come to terms with traditions instilled a long time ago by our forefathers. When it comes to social manifestos, such as love, marriage and commitment, the wedding ring is the most symbolic feature on anyone's hand and is easily recognizable even by little children. I have recently heard my friend's daughter utter in sheer joy the words "Hey, you two are married!" in her marshmallow voice when she noticed that me and my wife were wearing the same rings on our fingers. This made me think and realize that the wedding ring is one of the most easily recognizable trinkets that can be worn by a human being.

A brief history lesson

Wedding rings have been around since the ancient Romans. They believed that the vein in the ring finger led straight to the heart and that having a ring on it would give the wearer of the ring's counterpart a smooth, one-way high lane to your feelings. If this doesn't sound romantic, I don't know what does. Committing yourself to someone and trusting them isn't always easy, but those who find the way reward themselves with each other's compassion and sympathy for all eternity.

There are a lot of different types of wedding rings

Wedding rings nowadays can be customized to the littlest details and can be made to fit both the partners' liking. From personal messages engraved on the exterior or interior sides, to special fittings with precious minerals, to being custom built from start to finish into different shapes, sizes and even materials. Yes, there are people who like to forge their own wedding rings out of metals and/or other materials and they do so when the first possible opportunity arises, hoping that their partner will feel the same way and will, with all their loving hearts, say yes.

But in the end, wedding rings are just symbols

No matter what you have bought for your big day and how much customization you put into it yourself, wedding rings will always be just trinkets of commitment and love and unity. Don't fret about whether she'll like it or not, don't be scared to go a little overboard with the fancy and cheesy lines inside the ring and most definitely you can't go wrong with it if it's made of precious metals like gold, silver or platinum. Sure, a ring is still a ring, it needs to show respect and everlasting love for the one you'll give it to and it needs to show respect to yourself, too.

And those symbols you'll wear forever

When buying or making a custom ring, always remember why you are doing it in the first place and try not to get caught up in the haute-couture sense if you know for even one bit that your future spouse doesn't like it that much. Think about it as both of your promises to each other. Do you really want it to look as flashy as possible or do you want it to be tasteful and unique? Bottom line: be considerate.

How to buy your wedding bands

Now the two of you can begin the adventure of planning a wedding and choosing the right wedding bands for yourselves. The key with this purchase is to find the wedding bands that are right for you. They should be a reflection of your personalities and fit your lifestyle, as well as your budget. Ideally, you will be wearing these rings for the rest of your lives. These don't necessarily have to be a matching set, which is a growing trend in the wedding world.

Before you start browsing through the overwhelming choices in the myriad of jewelry stores, make a few decisions to help with shopping success. Begin by setting a budget. This isn't just a one-time expense. Most rings will require regular cleaning and maintenance, like recoating or polishing. You may also want to consider insurance on these rings as well as the engagement ring. Once you have both agreed on a budget and whether or not you want stones in these bands, it is time to shop.

If you are opting for stones in your wedding bands, review the 4C's so you are knowledgeable about your choices and specifications. There are also setting choices for stones, but the most popular band setting is the channel set, where stones are placed down into a groove around the ring.

There are four basic metal choices in wedding bands: yellow gold, white gold, titanium and platinum. Gold is rated in karats, which depend on the ratio of gold to other metals. Gold bands are actually alloys; the gold is mixed with other metals for strength, color and brilliance. There is usually 75% gold in an 18-karat ring. White gold is normally coated or plated with rhodium to give it a whiter, shinier finish. If you wear gold rings, they will eventually need to be recoated. Many jewelers will do this for free or a very minimal charge. Be sure to ask about this while shopping.

Titanium is growing more and more popular in wedding band choices. It is less expensive than platinum and very durable. Titanium rings will not dull, rust or corrode. They may need to be polished or buffed at some point to remove scratches, but their upkeep is minimal. Titanium rings can also come with an inlay of other metals, be stamped with a design, or engraved for a personal touch.

Platinum is a very popular metal choice. Like gold, platinum is an alloy, but it must be at least 90% pure to be marketed as platinum, otherwise it must be labeled as a platinum alloy. Platinum is stronger than gold and doesn't require any plating or coating to shine it or improve its brilliance.

Bridesmaids

Bridesmaids are an important part of any wedding. They are like the best friends of the bride. They help her with chores, comfort her when she is having second thoughts, console her when the center pieces don't look nearly the same as those that have been presented to her and last, but definitely not least, they party like there's no tomorrow and have a great time with the bride.

In the bridesmaid's game, everybody has something to do

Whether it's about running last-minute errands, or helping with pre-wedding things, an extra bridesmaid is always a useful one. Let's say you're the bridesmaid and you want to help. Keep a sharp eye on what would need to be done from the beginning and do your research before offering to help. You need to be very specific when you tell the bride you want to help and you need to do your job right, or else she might blame you if something goes wrong during the wedding.

To keep it simple, here's a list of things you can offer your help for.

Shop for bridesmaids dresses

Make sure to ask the bride if you're not sure what sort of wedding she is going for. There's nothing shameful in asking a question and nothing is worse than being in charge with dresses and buying ones that don't fit with the wedding's theme.

Help to plan, pay and be the co-host for the bridal shower and bachelorette party

After all, that's where all the nice single guys will be!

Offer to stand on the receiving line

You could stand in for the bride if she has urgent things to attend to.

Offer to keep the RSVP lists and help with invitations

If there's something really annoying to do when it comes to weddings, invitations take the cake. They need to be written to each person or couple and they need to be sent out, kept a record of, RSVPd, a record of the RSVP list kept and finally they need to look darn fantastic!

Keep track of the gifts that are received

Keeping a list of the gifts received and who they were was from will come in super handy when writing thank-you notes. The bride and groom will definitely appreciate your help on this one.

Help the matron or maid of honor with the bride's wedding gown train

Make sure to always keep an eye out and lend a hand if it becomes unhooked. Also, help the bride by bustling the train before dancing begins.

Emotional support

I can't stress this enough. Both the bride and the groom need plenty of people to show their support and appreciation for what they have decided. They need to feel safe with their decision and be happy with everything related to their wedding. Having a close friend supporting them always means a whole lot more than being just a bridesmaid. During their most stressful weeks, they will greatly appreciate your support.

Groomsmen

Groomsmen are the male equivalent of bridesmaids. They're the guys who have been there through thick and thin and now the time has come to support the one who got away and fell so deep in love that you wish someday you yourself will be this lucky. As a groomsman, you have responsibilities too. If we take them into account from the groom's point of view, they are pretty important ones, too.

Here's a list of what you can help with:

Always be there for the groom emotionally

This is a pretty stressful time for the groom and he needs someone to talk to before and during the wedding. Keeping an open mind and a calm attitude always helps and is guaranteed to help the groom feel more trusting in coming out to you with his deepest fears.

Be the ring bearer for the wedding

Ring bearers are the ones who hold and take care of the groom and bride's precious wedding rings until the vows have been exchanged. Please, for the sake of everyone's tickers, triple-check the place you keep the rings so that you won't give anyone any heart attacks.

Help organize the bachelor's party

Don't shy out if you have a good idea. The thing is, even the best man needs a little help from time to time, he's only human. What better place to make your presence felt than at the bachelor's party? Bring your ideas forward, speak your mind, and offer your insights on whether lager is better than regular beer or it's the other way around.

Sign the marriage license as the witness along with the maid of honor

Being the witness of a wedding and signing the marriage license is one thing that is always looked upon with good eyes and that will get you into other weddings as a groomsman or even the best man.

Help decorate the car in which the groom and bride will drive off into the sunset

Bring your cans and your most colorful sheets of paper and start cutting! Make noise! Stand out from the crowd and be sure that the "JUST MARRIED" sign is big enough for anyone to see. Get together with the other groomsmen and ask the bridesmaids for help in decorating the getaway ride. This is the most fun a man can have at a wedding, besides the bachelor's party.

Dance! Dance! Dance!

Dance with the bride, dance with the bride's mother, dance with the bridesmaids, dance your feet off whenever you get the occasion. This is a great way to get other people to join in and nobody likes a dull wedding where everyone just sits, eats and listens to the orchestra play a faint tune.

Help with the groom's wedding-wear

Give your opinion on what the groom is wearing and make suggestions based on research that you've conducted and make sure that everything about the c

Wedding Rehearsal

The wedding rehearsal has become a widespread tradition – and for good reason. Weddings can be complicated. Often the families of the bride and groom spend over a year planning the big day and it needs to go off without a hitch. Wedding ceremonies can be complicated and typically involve many individuals, who need to receive the right cues at the right time. Moreover, typically wedding parties consist of complete strangers – who are expected to appear comfortable with one another. The solution to this complicated situation is the wedding rehearsal.

The wedding rehearsal has two significant functions. The first is to allow members of the wedding party to practice before the big day – like they say, practice makes perfect. Secondly, the rehearsal dinner is a time for the family and friends of the bride and groom to get to know one another before the wedding day.

The Rehearsal

The wedding rehearsal can be a lot of fun, but it should also be taken seriously. If the couple has hired a wedding coordinator – the coordinator should be at the rehearsal and should run the show. The rehearsal should include everyone who will have a role in the wedding, even if it is a minor role. Thus, make sure to include ring bearers and flower girls. The rehearsal should be a "walkthrough" of the wedding. The wedding coordinator should place everyone in their "starting positions" and should provide them with their cues. Once the stage has been set, the wedding coordinator should begin the processional by signaling each member of the wedding party with their cue. This will allow the wedding party to become more comfortable with their roles in the ceremony and will be a chance to clarify any confusion.

The Rehearsal Dinner

The rehearsal dinner should be viewed as a meet and greet. This may be the first time members of the bride's family are meeting members of the groom's family. Therefore it is important to create a relaxed environment, where people can feel comfortable. Traditionally, the rehearsal dinner is hosted by the groom's parents. The guest list should include anyone who participated in the wedding ceremony rehearsal as well as close family and friends who are not part of the ceremony. It is customary for the groom's parents to give a short speech at the rehearsal dinner. However, it is common for representatives of both families to speak.

The Rehearsal Dinner Venue

First, the rehearsal dinner does not have to be a dinner at all. It is intended to be a fun affair for the two families to become better acquainted. Therefore, the "rehearsal dinner" can be a nice brunch or a late lunch. The venue for the rehearsal dinner should match the personalities of the bride and groom. This does not have to be a formal event and it should be as stress free as possible. Often, families will host the event at the couple's favorite restaurant, at the groom's parents' home or in a hotel banquet hall.

Wedding Flowers and Decorations

The first thing one notices when they walk into a wedding hall is the décor and the ambiance. Weddings halls can be used as outlets for expressing and capturing the personalities of the bride and groom – that is, if the flowers and decorations are done properly.

Decorating a wedding can be both daunting and costly. It is not uncommon for people to spend tens of thousands of dollars on flowers and decorations alone. However, there are many steps brides can take to cut costs and still have the picture perfect wedding they have been dreaming about since childhood.

Wedding Flowers

Floral arrangements are indeed beautiful, but hiring a florist to make them can be costly. There are a few ways you can save on floral arrangements – and still have the wedding of your dreams. First, consider recycling your flower arrangements. That is to say, take the flower arrangements that were used at the ceremony and transfer them to the reception hall. By doing this you can invest in quality flower arrangements without the double cost. Next, consider using flowers that are in season – getting flowers that are not in season can cost as much as five times more. For example, if your wedding is in the early spring you can save a lot of money by using tulips, which are beautiful in their own right. Finally, embrace the concept of less is more. Simple is elegant. Not only can cutting back on flowers be cheaper, but it can create a wonderfully elegant impression. This can be accomplished by only purchasing flowers for the essentials: bouquets, boutonnieres and altar arrangements.

Wedding Decorations

Who doesn't love going to a wedding with stunning wedding decorations? The right wedding decorations can really make a lasting impression. Fortunately, your wedding can make a lasting impression without costing you a fortune. Here are a few ideas. First, use the natural or existing décor of your venue. If the ceremony is in a church, survey the churches current décor. This way you can both highlight its beauty and utilize it for your own décor. If you are getting married outdoors, utilize nature. Create a focal point by placing the altar in the middle of two rows of trees, etc. Next, utilize candles. Candles are beautiful and romantic. Fill glass vases with water and float lit tea lights inside of them. This creates a very elegant look and costs very little. Additionally, use a theme to guide you. By choosing a theme you can create a masterpiece with very little. A Feng Shui theme, which creates balance and harmony, can be simply put together with a few bonsai trees dispersed along the aisle and a rock garden near the altar – creating a sense of calm and beauty. Finally, remember, simplicity is elegant and it can leave a lasting impression. Over decorating can be a costly mistake. Invest wisely in the right decorations but don't go overboard. Consider focusing your decorations on the altar, this will naturally draw everyone's attention in that direction.

Wedding Music

The music playing on your wedding day may not be as memorable to you as your first kiss after saying "I do", however it is guaranteed to be the most memorable part for your guests. Not to mention, that music is the key to tying together all the efforts you have invested into creating a magical wedding atmosphere. Therefore, don't forget to invest into picking the right band/DJ and selecting the right songs. When considering whether or not to hire a band, make sure you consult your check book – a band can easily cost $1,000 per member, i.e. 5 people in the band can cost $5,000 (not including food, transportation costs, etc.). However, the right band can make all of the difference in the world. If a band is not in your price range, don't panic – a good DJ can make for a magical evening.

What Kind of Song Do you Choose for the Ceremony

The processional music is the music that the wedding party will walk down the aisle to. There is no rule as to which song you must play or that you need to play the same song for everyone. This is entirely up to you. When choosing a song, make sure you keep in mind the atmosphere you are trying to create. Softer, slower music can create a warmer, loving feel. Whereas faster, louder music creates much excitement and energy. Traditionally, brides select slower music for the processionals – though not always the same song for everyone. One of the most common songs for brides to walk down to is Canon in D. This song is sweet, elegant and resonates with most people. After the ceremony (for the recessional), people often choose music which is more upbeat and has a faster tempo. At this point the bride and groom traditionally run down the aisle as a married couple – often having rice or flower petals tossed at them by their guests. Think about the type of music you would like, something that speaks to you as a couple. One of the more common choices is the Wedding March.

Reception Music

The music you choose to play at your reception will dictate the energy of your reception. The dancing and the schmoozing will all be influenced by the music you play. If you prefer to have slower music, then you will create an elegant atmosphere. Slower music selections typically mean slower dancing, while faster music typically creates a more relaxed and upbeat feeling - shoes usually come off as everyone goes to boogie to "Play that Funky Music." The most common practices is to create a blended environment by playing selections of both faster and slower music. Finally, this brings us to the most important song – the one that will be played during the couple's first dance. This song should be one that reflects the personalities of the bride and groom. It should be an expression of who they are. For some that means a slow dance and for others that means a choreographed performance.

Unforgettable Moments: Filming Your Wedding Ceremony

Your wedding day is a special occasion which you would want to remember for a very long time, if not forever. A collection of photographs will help you to hold the memory from that day in your mind. The main challenge with the photos is that they have to be really good, so that you will want to make an album and show it to your family and friends (or to your children) from time to time, or decorate one of the walls with them. The best advice will be to get a really good photographer who understands what you want.

Hire a professional

The wedding day is always about you and your significant other. Be sure that it is memorable by hiring a professional photographer who will do their job with style and heart. Be ready to pay a generous amount of money for a good professional photo shooting session, which might cost you from $1,000 and more — this depends on what you wish and whom you hire. Of course, you might ask a friend to be your photographer, but do this only if you are pretty sure about his or her candidacy. In the end, be prepared to offer them a reward, as every job must be paid. In any case, we suggest that you do not deprive your friend of an opportunity to enjoy the day with you and your guests, and that you hire a wedding photographer.

Choose your personal wedding photography style

Some like it casual. There is no better shot than a spontaneous one, in which you look relaxed, natural and unprepared. For example, it can be the photo of you two holding hands while walking to the wedding ceremony location. Casual is very nice too. Don't be too formal on the photos, but rather be lively and realistic. There is no rule, however, against the staged photos. Just avoid the clichés, and discuss your ideas with the groom and the photographer. Maybe one of them will suggest a better idea that you like more.

Select the setting

Choose the setting for the photo shoot. While in most cases it is the wedding location, you might have a favorite place where you want to have a couple of pictures together with your man. The range of scenes might vary; the common settings include nature, seashore, staircases, architectural objects, or the streets of your city. Usually, staged photos come along here, but you can also experiment with the environment: make use of the particular objects, interact with them, and show them as a part of your world.

Involve the people

There is no doubt that your guests should be present on the wedding photos too. Prepare for a series of group photos – they can range from the staged group portraits to the more non-standard solutions. The latter might involve using the same object by everybody on the photo. For example, put on sunglasses or tell your bridesmaids to wear the same-colored dresses, or simply hold a flower in your hands. The photographer might provide you with some ideas.

Be in harmony

Make sure the photos look natural. The wedding day is about harmony between the two people, so let it be seen in the photos. Be yourself and celebrate your freedom – the two of you are in the very center of everything, and the day revolves around you. There is no need to act or try to look something you're not. Be ready to experiment and to reveal your true creative selves. In the end, you will have the best documentation of the best day in your life.

Your Love Carriage, or Wedding Transportation Tips

You are planning a wedding ceremony, and one of the most important issues should be how you are going to get there. It all depends on your personal preferences, the style of the wedding you choose, the number of people you are inviting, and the distance between the main locations. While Limos and Rolls-Royces are the most classic choices, there are a lot of other alternatives you might want to consider. We'll just outline some essentials for you below.

Think about whom you are taking with you

The first thing you need to bear in mind when ordering wedding transportation is people you are going to take care of. How many of them will be there? How far do they live from the wedding location? How bad do you want everyone to be on time? These questions will help you to decide what kind of transportation you are going to arrange.

The most common choices are either taking the two of you to the ceremony separately or renting a car for more people. If you have decided on getting to the location as a couple, you will fit into a mini or a cabrio, or you can surprise everyone and arrive on horseback. Still, you might want to consider taking the photographer with you to make a few shots while on the road.

If you do want a bigger company with you, then go for it. While you and bridesmaids will perfectly fit into a neat sedan, there are also the groom and his groomsmen that you might want to fit into one car. If you are willing to take more people with you, then a bigger vehicle is needed. For larger numbers of people, minivans or shuttle buses are often used.

Make the best from your car rental

When booking a car (or cars) for your wedding ceremony, be sure to make it in advance. Although there are a variety of companies, they may turn out to be all booked closer to your wedding date. Moreover, if you book for June in January, there is a good chance that you will get an early bird discount.

Many wedding car rental companies often have discounts for those who arrange transportation for not just one occasion (the wedding ceremony itself), but also for engagement or bachelorette parties. You just have to make sure that you are using the same company on all the mentioned occasions.

Also, if you are booking a car, you are paying for a certain amount of time. If it's a really short way from your home to the wedding ceremony location, better make the best of the rent time by, say, making a few circles around the town — this can surely add to the overall festive mood!

Be creative

Although transportation seems like a very earthly issue, you can be creative here too. It all depends on your personal preferences and the financial resources you possess. You can take a romantic ride in a carriage or make an entrance on horseback, provided that you will be able to hold still on the animal. If your dress can allow this, you may think about riding a bike — a vintage one, with a basket of flowers at the front. If you are using car rental services, it's not necessary to book classic vehicles — thankfully, there are enough companies that will help you to stand out. A vintage Vespa, a Volkswagen hippie van, a double-decker tour bus — whatever your heart may desire! Make your arrival at the ceremony memorable!

Getting Your Marriage License

A marriage requires a permit which you and your fiancé should obtain in order to get married. This is a formality to ensure that your intention to marry is based on your free and good will and that you recognize your responsibilities in front of each other. To get the license, you will need to collect some papers and wait some time before it's okay to throw a wedding. Below is some information you will need to know about the marriage license.

What is the application procedure?

The first thing that you need to do after you get engaged is to set the date of your wedding. You will need to know this in order to plan your visit to the town's authority for a marriage license. The problem is that it has an expiration date which can be up to six months, so there is no need to rush for the document immediately after the engagement.

The license can be obtained at the town hall or at a local marriage license bureau. Usually, they have limited working hours, and you should make yourself familiar with those before arriving there in person. It is better to call the respective authority and ask for the details. It might happen that you will have to make an appointment before paying them a personal visit. Besides, the bureau will provide you with a list of documents you need to apply for a license — the set of papers can vary depending on your location and/or place of residence.

What are the documents?

The usual set of documents you need for your marriage license application is different across the countries and states. Some will have more strict requirements than others. Below, we have collected a full list of documents that will suffice everywhere around the US and in most countries as well.

1. Proof of residence or citizenship (passport or ID will definitely work here).

2. Birth certificate (it serves as a proof of your age).

3. Photo ID.

4. Parental consent, only if you or your fiancé is under the age of consent.

5. Divorce decree (it applies only if you were married before).

6. Death certificate (if you are a widower).

7. Blood test results. They are necessary in some states, but not everywhere. Make sure that you do the test beforehand, so that you have the results with you on the day that you apply for the marriage license.

What next?

Having collected all the necessary documents, you will have to wait for a certain amount of time until you get the license and can get married. In most cases, the time span between obtaining of the license and the wedding day is half a month to half a year. During that time, you are free to get married.

Still, it won't be over yet. After you both have signed the license at the wedding, you will need to have it sent to the local bureau, and they will send you its certified copy back. Usually this takes several weeks, but it can also last for a few months. The license will serve you not just as a proof of your marriage, but also as a reminder of the mutual responsibilities as well as long happy days of marriage to come.

How to Not Forget Anything with a To-do List

Once you've had a marriage proposal, you are believed to be engaged. This means that you are entering a very delicate period of your life as a couple which involves a lot of planning and decision-making. There will be several milestones on your way from the engagement to the wedding that you will need to take care of. Make sure that you've successfully passed them by crossing the things off your wedding to-do list. We have outlined the checklists for the following periods: 12 months before the wedding, 6 months, a month, a week, a day before, the wedding day, and post-wedding.

A year before the wedding

Once you have got engaged, draw up a sketch of what your wedding will look like. If you want a celebration, it is the time to think of the date and to plan your budget beforehand, so that you have the necessary amount of money for the ceremony. When planning, surfing the Internet for prices and options will come in handy. Think of the guests you will want to see at the celebration. Maybe an engagement party will be the place where you make an announcement and verbal invitations to the people. Just don't forget to send the written invitations as well – at this point, you don't have to be specific about the time and date.

6 months before the wedding

By that time, you should have chosen the bridal gown you are going to wear on your wedding day. At this point, you should interview and maybe hire wedding professionals who will help you to go through the whole process with little or no pain. It is also time to select the theme, book the venue, transportation, order the bridesmaids' dresses, and research the accommodation for guests. You can book your honeymoon trip too, so that you can get the best holiday offer.

After this, you can make yourself busy with reserving cooks and food for the celebration. Don't forget to buy the wedding rings, gifts for the parents, guests, and each other. It is about time to send out the beautifully written invitations via mail. Optional but useful: attend a bridal shower to have a little fun with your friends amidst the planning hassle.

1 month before the wedding

The most important thing is to obtain a marriage license, after which you will be able to return to the planning. You might want to draft out a wedding program to entertain the guests. Speaking of guests, you need to make the final RSVP list. At this stage, you can book a stylist and a makeup artist, and maybe have a trial run. Then, make the arrangements with the photographer (and videographer, if necessary).

1 week before the wedding

Take care of your look and have your hair cut. Once refreshed, you can visit the host/reception, the list of guests, plan their seating and make the name cards for every attendee. Make the final arrangements with the catering, cooks, musicians, transportation service, etc. Have bachelor/bachelorette parties. Closer to the wedding, you will need to set the time and date of guests' pickups.

1 day before the wedding

Have your wedding gown pressed and ready. The groom should have his suit ready as well. The last day before the wedding is good for paying all the checks and learning about the procedure of covering the additional costs. You should also get all the emergency phone numbers, just in case, to be sure everything is under control. Rehearse the speeches and the ceremony — it's always better to know what to do and when in advance. Bring out the decorations and set the scene for the big day. Don't forget to hand the wedding license to the officiant.

The wedding day

Present and exchange the gifts. Introduce everyone to one another and appoint a person to maintain contact with the photographer and the reception site manager. The maid of honor and the best man should receive wedding bands to hold at the ceremony. Enjoy your wedding day!

Post-wedding checklist

After the wedding celebration is over, make sure that you have paid any unpaid costs, returned the gown and the suit to the rental, and written thank-you notes to all the guests who attended and to the personnel who were really helpful and professional. In the end, make sure that you have nothing left on your to-do list and go for your well-deserved honeymoon trip.

ATTENDANTS AND GUESTS

Choosing Your Wedding Attendants

Choosing the attendants in your bridal party is one of the most important, and perhaps most difficult, wedding decisions you will make. Obviously you will want to include family members and friends to whom you feel the closest. While it's tempting to fill the wedding party with your own family and friends, be sure to include those from the groom's side of the family as well. Very shortly, they will be your family too, and you want to start off on the right foot.

The Maid (or Matron) of Honor is responsible for the details of the bridal shower as well as the bachelorette party, if you choose to have one. Not a fan of bachelorette parties? Try something different like a pajama party, complete with pizza, chocolate, and a DVD of your favorite romantic comedy.

Your Maid of Honor should be the absolutely closest woman in your life, often a sister, cousin, or best friend. The ideal candidate should have a nicely balanced responsible and fun-loving personality. She will be in charge of helping with various pre-wedding activities, such as bridesmaid dress fittings, addressing invitations, and anything else the bride needs help with. Traditionally, there is only one Maid of Honor, but it's your wedding, so do what's best for you.

The Best Man is the equivalent of the Maid of Honor. He is the groom's brother, cousin, or best friend. He must have at least a bit of responsibility, as he will be holding the rings and planning the bachelor party. Most men want a crazy bachelor party, but for those who don't, a night out at a sports event is a great substitution. The bachelor party should not take place the night before the wedding. A hung over groom and groomsmen do not fit in with a bride's vision of the perfect wedding!

Bridesmaids and groomsmen will also be favorite friends and family. There is no right or wrong answer to how many of these attendants are present. Be sure to choose attendants who are not overly dramatic, and do not pair two people who do not get along. Sticking to these principles will save you many hours of needless drama and stress.

These attendants will also need to be present at pre-wedding functions and help with all the small details, such as decorating the reception venue (if you choose to do this yourself), addressing invitations, and the like.

The children attendants can be one of the most delightfully fun wedding choices. Typically three to six years of age, the ring bearer and flower girl are nieces or nephews, brothers or sisters, or your own children. The ring bearer will hold a pillow (or something more creative) with the wedding rings secured with ties so they cannot be lost, and the flower girl carries a basket of flower petals, scattering them on the floor as they walk down the aisle.

The flower girl and ring bearer often cause disruption due to their young age, but rather than taking away from the loveliness of the wedding ceremony, they add a sweetness that will be remembered by the wedding party and guests alike for years to come.

Your wedding ceremony is your own unique vision, which is different from every other bride and groom. Be true to yourselves, make the choices you both desire, and you will have the day of perfection from your dreams.

Family

Ah, family. The people who love you more than anyone else in the world. Ironically, these are the same people who know which buttons to push to annoy you and send you into fits of anger.

Be warned, these people will add their two cents into every wedding choice you try to make. Attempting to align everyone in two families (and more, if there are step-parents involved) is not a feat easily accomplished. There are ways, however, to make the stress less present.

At the very beginning, have talks with separate sides of the family and set guidelines for behavior. You think your parents, or your future in-laws, are the sweetest people to grace this earth? Possibly, but wedding planning can bring out the worst in some people, and you want to have certain rules in place before the drama begins.

Explain that you and your fiancé will try in every way to include them in the details of the ceremony planning, but ultimately the choices will be finalized by the bride and groom. Reassure all parties involved that you respect their opinion and want their input, but it is simply impossible for each person to have their way. Rejecting a thought or idea is not the same as rejecting the person it came from.

To circumvent hurt feelings, explain that while you understand each person only means the best and wants your wedding to be wonderful, the final results need to align with the vision of the bride and groom. Don't allow your mother, who eloped to the courthouse for a quick wedding and wants better for you, to push you into decisions you don't want to make.

Perhaps your father wants to walk you down the aisle, but your stepfather was the one who was always there for you. Guilt is a horrible emotion, and has no place in the wedding scenario. Either allow them both to walk you down the aisle, or choose your stepfather if he is the one you really wish to do the honors. You can give your father a different place, such as the father/daughter dance at the reception.

These types of issues will happen, but it does not have to ruin the fun in planning your wedding, or the relationship that is being tested. If you lay down the law beforehand, it should help things run more smoothly.

Remember that the anger and jealousy that may pop up stem from hurt feelings of family members that feel left out or ignored. It doesn't really have anything to do with the ceremony itself, but the place they are afraid of losing in your life. Be kind, though firm, when dealing with these problems, and you will avert wedding, as well as relational, disasters.

Guests

When sitting down with your fiancé over hot coffee or a refreshing iced tea, a blank tablet or screen before you waiting to be filled with names of prospective wedding guests, there are a few guidelines to discuss before you dive in.

First of all, you want to decide if you are basing your guest list on the chosen venue, or if the venue depends on the amount of guests you plan to invite. Once you have those facts ironed out, you can begin the guest list.

Next you will want to divide the guest list into portions. This can be done a few different ways. The bride's family can take half, and the groom's the other half. The bride and groom can be responsible for half the list, while delegating each parental group with a quarter of the remaining portion, or it can be divided equally in thirds. However you divvy up the list, do it early on, so everyone knows where they stand and there will be less drama and stress involved.

The beginning of the list is easy, as this will be dedicated to the must-have family members and friends that you each agree must be invited. The rest of the list becomes more challenging as you wade through distant relatives, coworkers, church family, and your favorite waitress at the nearby diner.

It is a good idea to set certain limits to determine whether or not a potential guest should be invited. Perhaps you want to draw the limit at friends you have not seen or talked to in over a year. You can expand this to two or three years if you wish. Of course, there may be exceptions to this rule, such as a close friend who lives far away. But you get the general idea. Set limitations that will make your choices easier, and stick to them!

Some brides like to create two lists: One for guests that absolutely must be included, and a back-up list of people to be invited if you have enough space left in your venue, or you have a large number of guests that cannot attend.

Send the first round of invitations out early so you have plenty of time to mail the second round of invitations without being overly obvious that these guests are your second choice.

Yet another way to form your guest list is to brainstorm with your fiancé and write down the names of every person you would like to invite. Then go through and eliminate the names you don't have room to accommodate.

Whichever way you choose to go about building your guest list, try to be courteous and understanding of the other parties involved. You each have people in mind that you wouldn't dream of excluding. Be tolerant of one another's decisions, and your guest list preparation can be an enjoyable activity.

Invitations and Stationery

Whether you are going with elegantly printed invitations and envelopes addressed by a calligrapher, or simple do it yourself projects printed from your own computer, choosing the wedding invitations and stationery is definitely one of the most fun and creative of the wedding preparations.

The invitation ensemble generally includes the invitation, of course, as well as a reply card and envelopes. If you wish, other items such as reception cards, maps, and directions can also be added.

If you prefer to go with traditionally printed invitations and stationery, there are tons of designs from simple to elaborate, with a plethora of different font styles, colors, and backgrounds to choose from.

Or you can decide to showcase your creative skills by designing and printing the invitations and stationery yourself. It can be a fun way to put your own personal stamp on the wedding. This also includes a large variety of font and color samples, as well as many backgrounds.

Allow your invitations to echo the style of your wedding. If the ceremony will be traditional and elegant, the stationery and wording of the invitations should be elegant as well. Incorporate the colors of the wedding into the cards and/or envelopes. If the big day will be an exciting celebration in a rainbow of color, then by all means, allow that to shine through in your stationery.

However you choose to go about inviting your guests, make it a fun and relaxing time. So many wedding decisions are surrounded in stress, but choosing the invitations should not be one of them.

Gift Ideas for the Wedding Party

Let's face it, your wedding is all about you, and the wedding party understands that and gives their best efforts toward making your day the best one of your life. They have bought expensive clothing and accessories, taken time out of their own busy schedules to fulfill all wedding party responsibilities, and provided a shoulder to cry on when the tension became too much to take. They deserve a small token of appreciation for that kindness, don't they?

Setting a budget early on will determine the price you can spend on your attendants. Even a low budget can result in lovely gifts; you just may need to be more creative.

You might decide to give your bridal party matching gifts that can be worn during the wedding. Just be sure that it's something they will treasure and be able to use afterwards, as well. Matching bracelets or earrings, a lovely little clutch, or matching necklaces are a good bridesmaid gift that will continue to please them long after the ceremony has come and gone.

Perhaps you prefer to grace your attendants with something that is more personal. Personalized gifts such as monogrammed wine glasses, tote bags, or lockets make a beautiful gift that most bridesmaids and maids of honor will treasure.

For something more unique, check out local craft shows or Renaissance festivals for handmade goodies like scented soaps or candles, original jewelry, wind chimes, paintings, or even a fun caricature of each bridesmaid.

A more expensive gift is not necessarily a better one. If your budget for wedding party gifts is on the lower side, there are many items you can put together or make by hand that will have greater meaning and sentimental value than anything you could buy.

Purchase a variety of fun picture frames, and make sure that you have taken recent selfies with each person in the bridal party, or have your fiancé subtly snap some pictures during wedding planning get-togethers. Whether you want to go with serious or goofy photos, a picture of yourself with the attendant will show how much she means to you, and will be something she will treasure for years to come. It's also a wonderful way to highlight the memories you've made together during the wedding preparations.

Finding gifts for the groomsmen can be a more challenging feat to accomplish. These gifts can include tickets to a sports event, a monogrammed beer mug or flask, personalized money clip or wallet, an autographed picture of his favorite sports player or team, or a nice watch.

Gifts for flower girls and ring bearers should be fun and simple to shop for. Children in the three to six year old range are pretty easy to please, for the most part.

Think of flower girls as mini bridesmaids. Girls like the same feminine things as women do. A necklace and bracelet combo can be personalized in many ways. A simple initial or entire monogram is perfect, or maybe a locket that says flower girl. Hair accessories, personalized tote bag or t-shirt, or even a girly camera that she can use to take her own wedding photos would surely be appreciated by this sweet little girl.

Perhaps finding a child's ring in the fashion of the bride's wedding ring would bring great joy to the flower girl who dreams of her own future wedding.

Are ring bearers as tricky to please as the grown up groomsmen? Surely that depends on the boy. A baseball engraved with your ring bearer's name would make a nice addition to his room décor, or a t-shirt with words "ring security" can serve to remind him of the important job he held during your special day.

However you choose to honor your attendants, be sure to put a lot of thought into the gifts. You want your appreciation to show. Give your wedding party words of gratitude as well. Take the time to let each one know how special they are to you and your fiancé, and that all their hard work has been noticed.

Give the gifts to your wedding party at a time when you are not busy with anything else. Book a nice pre-wedding luncheon or invite them to your home for a home cooked meal. The extra effort will be worth it to make them feel special.

DRESS AND LOOK

The Importance of the Dress and Look

For many brides, the dress can be the most important part of the whole wedding. It is easy to see why this can be the case: as children, from an early age, we are encouraged to dream about our ideal wedding dress and how it will work. It is not unusual for young women to have an idea of the kind of wedding dress they would like even before they are in a serious relationship. It can be one of the most talked about elements of the wedding afterwards, too – one of the most urgent questions on the lips of those who were not there will be, what was the dress like?

Choosing a look for the overall wedding can have a real influence on its success. It is important that you make the decision to choose a look rather than picking each piece without thinking about it. You need to be able to tie everything together, so that nothing looks out of place. It would be unfortunate if your bridesmaids looked odd compared to your wedding dress, or your groomsmen were dressed differently to the groom. There does not have to be a particularly lavish or specific theme for your look. You just have to have something in mind, which will give you a direction to go in.

Once the event is over, the dress will sit in your wardrobe, swathed in bags to keep it clean and safe from moths. You will be getting it out every now and then to try it on and remembering how much you loved wearing it on the day. It is not unusual for a bride to cry the first time she tries on her dress, realizing that she has achieved her dream. The dress can be the pivotal part of the whole ceremony.

Not only that, but it has a bearing on the reception as well, especially if you are planning an outfit change. It is a common choice for the bride to find a dress which can be adapted from the day ceremony into the evening do. You will want to wear the full gown for your first dance together as well as the speeches, but after this you may want to be able to take part of the dress off to make it easier to move around. Having a coat or an overskirt which can be removed to create a lighter and smaller dress may be a good option.

Whatever you go for, it has to be something that works for the full day, and fits with an overall theme. For example, if your wedding theme is soft pastel colors, then being daring and going for a red dress or black bridesmaids' outfits just would not work. The same goes for the colors of waistcoats, jacket linings, pocket handkerchiefs, buttonholes, and flowers for the wedding party. It all has to be planned well. This could be the most important decision that you make.

Wedding Gown

We could probably fill an entire book with information on how to choose your wedding gown, and what types of dress there are for you to choose from. Here we have just the space of one chapter, so we are going to rush you through this topic as clearly as we can. You need to choose the color of your dress, the style of your dress, and of course fit it in to your budget. Your best option is to choose the kind of dress that you want first, and then try to find something that matches your dream within your budget.

You can start off by looking at the general shape. There are three types of dress you could go for when you boil it down to the essential elements. The first is a tea dress, of the type which was very popular in the 1950s. This is a shorter style, but has a lot of appeal because it is a very flattering shape. The second is a full-length gown, which can be either formfitting, straight, or A line. Finally, you can go for a ball gown shape, often referred to as a princess gown because of the width. It is entirely up to you what kind of dress you go for. You can read bridal magazines in order to find out what is in fashion at the moment if you like. This can help you to choose something which is very much in style. On the other hand, you may wish to go with something that speaks to your heart in terms of being the look you have always dreamed of.

In terms of color, you need to choose something which suits your color scheme and also fits well with a wedding dress. While you can go for a non-traditional color, normally a shade of white is preferred. There are different tones within this color, so do not imagine that it is as simple as it seems. Champagne, ivory, and off white are some of the most popular choices. If you are having trouble with visualizing these choices, your best option will be to go down to a bridal boutique and have a look at some of them in the flesh. Your computer monitor may not be calibrated properly, so looking at them online is not the best choice. Fabric can make a difference too. Chiffon, lace, silk, and tulle may be some of the choices that you consider, as they can affect the whole look of the dress.

When you have these ideas in mind, start searching the internet. You can find stores which stock hundreds of different styles, and you can easily sort them by the ideas that you have already decided on. This will help you to narrow it down. You can also go to boutiques and try on dresses in person. Eventually you will find your ideal style. Then it is a case of finding something within your budget that is very similar!

Bridal Salons

It is very important that you find a bridal salon that you are able to travel to. If you are tempted to find the best salon in the country or state, and travel there on a regular basis, you should be advised that this is a bad idea. It is only possible if you are going to travel in a way that does not stretch your budget. You may need to make several trips to and from your salon – one to try on a dress, at the very least, before you choose. You may need three or four before you find your dream dress. Then two or three more visits may be needed to get the adjustments needed, with one final appointment to try on the finished dress and collect it.

The salon that you choose will of course have an impact on the dress that you wear on the day. The reason why most brides go to a salon, rather than ordering online, is in order to make sure that their dress fits well. It can also give you an idea of the kind of dress that suits you if you do not yet have an idea of what you want. Most salons will have a range of dresses from different designers available. In more rare cases, you may be able to visit a salon which creates their own styles. It is likely that dresses made in-house are going to be a little more expensive. Alterations are almost always made in-house by a seamstress who is part of the business.

If you have a budget in mind for your dress, and it is one that you must stick to, then keep this in mind early on. Most salons will be able to give you an idea of the upper and lower limits of the dresses that they stock. Therefore, you can choose a salon which is within your price range. Try to go for a place that caps out at your maximum budget for the dress. This is because they will always want to show you their best pieces, and if they are out of your budget range, you risk falling in love with something that you cannot afford. If you do find something you love which is not within your range, try to negotiate. It may be that you can find a way to reduce the price. Perhaps they offer money off discount to those who refer friends who are getting married soon. It may be that they have a very similar style from the previous season left over that they are selling at a lower price. Be open with your bridal salon and explain to them that you simply cannot afford the price on the tag. Since it is their job to make the sale, they may be willing to try and accommodate you.

The assistants at the salon will know about wedding dresses better than anyone else you meet. Take their advice if you are unsure of what to wear.

Bride's Shoes and Accessories

After you have chosen the dress, and not before, you should start to think about shoes and accessories. The reason that you think about these things after you have already decided on your dress is because everything needs to match. There is no good getting a pair of shoes first, then having to work backwards to find a dress that accommodates them. You may end up paying a huge amount of money for designer shoes, only to fall in love with a dress that is full-length and would cover them completely. The same is true of accessories, which include jewelry, garters, tights, your bridal lingerie, a veil, and tiara.

Many people find that they can draw inspiration from those around them for their accessories in many ways. You will of course have heard the saying "Something old, something new, something borrowed, something blue". The idea is that you should wear at least one of each of the types of items mentioned on your wedding day. The new thing can easily be your dress, and then it is down to your accessories to provide the others. Many brides like to wear a blue garter, as it is hidden away and will not ruin the look of the outfit. It will also be a nice surprise for your husband on the wedding night.

In terms of something old, a favorite pair of earrings or piece of jewelry can fit the bill. You can even go for a pair of tights that you have had for a while, so long as they are good quality and will suit the rest of your wedding outfit. Something borrowed is traditionally taken from a member of your family, such as the mother of the bride, who will volunteer something from their own wedding. This could be a vintage tiara, a bracelet or necklace, or something more subtle that you can hide away on your person.

Make sure that you stick to a budget. Just getting a tiara and a pair of earrings can blow the budget for your accessories if you do not choose carefully. It is more important that you stick to your wedding budget than to have the loveliest pair of earrings. Consider your outfit and the requirements that it may provide. For example, if you are going to have your hair down, earrings may not be important. Similarly, a full-length sleeve gown might preclude the need for a bracelet. A veil is a traditional wedding accessory, but it is not absolutely essential, particularly if you are having a non traditional wedding. You can also skip the tiara – or go for a full size crown. It is all down to the theme of your wedding and the kind of look that you want. You can even style your jewelry around your chosen wedding rings if you want to pay real attention to detail. This can give the whole wedding more of a focus.

Bride's Hair

Getting your hair right can be very important. Most brides will choose to have a professional hairdresser come to them on the morning of the wedding to prepare their hair. If your budget doesn't stretch that far, you may consider having a friend or family member take over the duties. Either way, you must consider having a trial beforehand. In fact, neglecting to have a trial may open you up to the possibility of it all going wrong on the day. Although it will cost a little bit extra to have a trial done, it is one of the stages of preparation which you should not miss out.

The way it works is that you hire a hairdresser before the day of the wedding. You may choose them from looking at their online profile, or you may have a hairdresser that you already know. It could even be that you ask a friend who was married recently to tell you their recommendation. Whatever the case may be, once you have decided who you want to hire, you should have a consultation with them. During this session you discuss what kind of hair you would like to have. You can have it straight, curly, down, up, or a combination. You can also have it put into an elaborate style if you wish to be more impressive. This is a decision which should take into account the theme of your wedding and the style of your dress. Ideally you should be able to find the perfect hairstyle which brings the two together.

When you have decided on what you want, it is time to have a trial. You can have this just a few weeks before the wedding so that everything is fresh in your mind. Your hairdresser will do your hair and perhaps that of your bridesmaids if you wish, just the way that they would do it on the day. Then you take a look in the mirror, perhaps take a few photos, and see whether you like it. If you are not a fan, you can always do another trial with a different style. You can even try a different hairdresser if you are not happy with what they have done.

If the trial is successful, you are ready to finalize your plans for your wedding hair. You do not have to cover the hair for the bridesmaids, though it will certainly make them look better on the day if you do. If your budget doesn't allow it, you can ask them to cover it themselves. You should be able to get a discount on the day for a larger number of bridesmaids. Your hairdresser will want to cover everyone without forcing you to pay so much that you go elsewhere. However, if you are doing a small number of bridesmaids, you are likely to have to pay full price. You should certainly respect the hairdresser's rates, and do not expect a discount just because you ask for one.

Bridesmaids' Attire, Shoes, Accessories

When the bride has been sorted out, you still need to take care of the bridesmaids. It is customary to have all of the bridesmaids, including the maid of honor, dressed in matching outfits. You can allow some variation in a few cases. If one of the bridesmaids is very young, or very old, or pregnant, then you can change things up for their outfit. This will help you to ensure that the look and theme of the wedding remains consistent through your bridesmaids as well.

Whatever the color theme is for your wedding, this should be reflected in your bridesmaids' dresses. Normally it is the responsibility of the bridesmaids to pay for their own dresses, although you may choose to cover it yourself if you have room in your budget. Because of this, you should not go for an option which is too expensive, as it may not be possible for all of them to afford it. They should be purchased from the same shop, ensuring that you have the same dress with the same level of quality.

The full outfit has too much, so they should have new shoes to match the dresses as well. The same situation as before applies when it comes to paying for them. They shoes should preferably be in a neutral color, or reflect the color scheme. Younger children who are acting as bridesmaids can wear flat shoes instead of heels in the same color and approximate style. If a bridesmaid is very pregnant, you may wish for them to wear flats as well.

Accessories can normally be kept to a minimum. They may accessorize with their own jewelry, so long as they do not go too over the top or disregard the color scheme. You should bring this up with them before the ceremony to ensure that they have planned everything out in advance. They can also have small handbags in the same fabric and color as their dresses if you feel that it is appropriate. Other than this, the only thing they need is their flowers.

To get the dresses, you should ideally bring all of the bridesmaids together on one outing. This will allow you to get them all in the same place at the same time. Then they can all try on the same dress in their own respective sizes. This will allow you to see how it looks on all of them, ensuring that you make a choice that is flattering for the whole party. If you need to have any adjustments made, this may be carried out by the boutique if you have purchased them from a wedding specialist. If you buy them from a mainstream high-street retailer, you may have to take them to a specialist dress shop for alterations. This will undoubtedly cost more, so finding them in the right size straight away is recommended. Even if it takes a while to get something that suits everyone, it will be worth it.

Groom's Attire, Shoes, Accessories

Just like the bride, the groom needs to look his best on the day. It is normal for him to wear a suit, usually custom-made or tailored to his exact measurements. You may wish to hire a tuxedo, and it is perfectly acceptable to do this. On the other hand, you may wish to keep the suit afterwards, just as the bride keeps her dress. It is down to personal preference here. Tradition also dictates that the groom may wear traditional dress of his ancestors. For example, a Scottish groom may choose to wear a kilt. It should be made in the tartan of his clan.

Just as with the dress, it is not acceptable to leave buying your suit until the last minute. You need to start looking around fairly soon after you have announced your engagement. You should at least begin to get an idea of what kind of suit you will be looking for. Would you like a colored waistcoat, or a plain one? Will you wear a pocket handkerchief as well as a buttonhole? Do you require a top hat to go with it? Will you choose the standard black coloring, or go with grey? You should also consider whether you are going to hire or buy. This may be down to budget considerations, especially if you end up going over budget somewhere else.

When you are getting closer to the wedding, it is time to pick out your suit. The best option is to go to a proper gentleman's tailor in order to have it made to the correct measurements. They should provide adjustments if the finished article is not quite correct, but most professional tailors can get the job done in one take. It is important to consider the groomsmen as well, though do not feel that you have to base your choice of wardrobe on theirs. Once the suit is taken care of, you need to move on to shoes and accessories.

The top hat is not always considered these days, particularly since you will need to remove the hat once you are in the church or registry office. However, some gentlemen feel that it is a reflection of their own style, particularly if they are marrying or holding the reception at a country estate. You can reflect the color scheme in your pocket handkerchief, your waistcoat, and lining of your jacket if appropriate. Shoes should always be kept formal. Brogues are certainly acceptable, and dress shoes are the norm. They should normally be kept shined and clean for the big day. A handsome and perhaps expensive watch will top off the whole ensemble. Do not forget to wear a pair of nice cufflinks on your shirt, as this is a small detail which can be overlooked. No other accessories are necessary unless you want to add to your outfit. This is up to you and will be based on your own personal style and taste.

Groom's Hair

Most men do not even consider the fact that they might need to get themselves looking their best on the day. After all, women always go to the trouble of doing their hair and having their make-up done, no matter what the occasion is. For men, taking a formal approach to hair care can often mean just a simple cut every few weeks. They may not think beyond this, but this is a mistake and can damage the way they look on their wedding day. Remember that we do not just have to consider hair on the head, but facial hair as well.

If you do not normally wear a beard, then it is absolutely not appropriate to have one for your wedding day. You should be clean shaven in order to appear the most presentable in your wedding photos. This also gives the impression that you have made an effort, even if it is something that is part of your daily routine. If you do normally sport a beard, simply make sure that it is well trained and well kept. Having a barber's appointment a few days before the ceremony should be enough. Then simply carry out a quick bit of maintenance in the morning to ensure that everything is as it should be.

When it comes to your hair, consider carefully the style that you wish to wear. If you normally gel it up in spikes, this may not be appropriate for your wedding ceremony. Many grooms choose to take the formal approach, going for a hairstyle which is perhaps reminiscent of a bygone era. If your normal hairstyle is formal and smart looking enough, there is no need to change anything. Just make sure that your hair is cleanly washed and not greasy. Do not use too much product – and remember not to panic. If you start to think that you have gone wrong, just wash it out and start again. Cutting your hair yourself on the day or trying out something you have never done before is an absolute no-no.

If you feel that you need a bit more of a premium approach, you can book yourself a barber or hairdresser who will come down to you on the day of the ceremony. Since the bride is expected to do this, there is no reason why you should not as well. This will ensure that you look your absolute best, both to give you more confidence in yourself, and also to ensure that you can look back on the wedding photos with pride. While it can be funny to look back on embarrassing shots in 20 years time, the interval will not be as comfortable. You will certainly regret it if you do not take the time to consider this vital part of your appearance. With the ready availability of guides on the Internet, you can always look up appropriate hairstyles before the big day in order to get some idea of your approach.

Groomsmen's Attire, Shoes, Accessories

Just as with the bridesmaids, you also have to think about the other side of the wedding party as well. Your groomsmen need to be dressed smartly, preferably in matching suits, with the shoes and accessories to match. It is essential that everything is planned before the event, as it will not do simply to have them all turning up in their own suits which may not fit well and may be out of date. Remember that it is better to have them matching the color theme as well as everyone else. Just like with the bridesmaids, they are normally responsible for their own expenses, and so you may need to take this into account when you are choosing suits so that everyone will be able to afford it properly.

They do not have to have the exact same suit bought from the same shop, nor do their suits have to be bought new. So long as they all have a well fitted suit in the right color, you can just update them with some small touches. A waistcoat in the right color would fit the job, as would a new tie and pocket handkerchief. They will of course have buttonholes to wear on the day, which will be picked out to match the flowers. They may also wear hats if you feel that this is appropriate, though it is by no means necessary.

There is no real limit to the amount of groomsmen that you may have, but around three or four is generally best as a maximum. This is to minimize expenses, for them as well as yourselves – remember you will need to buy them all a present. They are the side of the wedding party who will be looking after the groom. It is important that they all look smart – a group of men in this situation when left to their own devices can often end up looking scruffy or mismatched. Take charge of this matter early on and ensure that everyone has something to go to the wedding in.

Each groomsman will need to escort a bridesmaid, so you should think about this also when picking out their color schemes. It is most appropriate to have the ties and pocket handkerchiefs of the groomsmen matching the color of the bridesmaids' dresses. This will make everything look better matched, and provide a better impression overall. You can also match up their buttonholes and bouquets. If you are thinking about having a slightly different shade for each bridesmaid, the same should be done for the groomsmen. This gives the impression that the change was made on purpose, rather than an accident caused by poorly chosen dresses.

Above all it is important that the groomsmen look smart. Their attire does not need to be expensive, but they should certainly look the part. Alterations can be made if necessary to ensure that their clothes are well fitting. Having shoes shined on the day is a good idea too.

Parents' Attire

It is very important that the parents are looked after. They are going to be in the spotlight almost as much as the bride and groom. For this reason, they are likely to need brand-new outfits, rather than sticking with something they already have in their wardrobe. This means two new pairs of suits and two new formal dresses need to be bought. In most cases, this will be their own financial responsibility, as the parents of the bride and groom pay for many aspects of the wedding traditionally. This means that it is a real weight off your mind.

However, there is still some discussion to be had. You should try to make sure that they are aware of the color scheme and theme of your wedding. They may wish to dress accordingly, coordinating themselves so that they match everyone else. If you have two colors in your theme, you can use this to creative effect. For example, if your colors are purple and gold, then you could split them between the two sets of parents. The parents of the bride could wear purple in their dress and suit, while the parents of the groom could wear gold. This will make a neat reference to the joining of your two families, as well as ensuring that everyone is well coordinated.

It is important that they are made to feel as much a part of the ceremony as possible. This is a very emotional time for them as they are watching their children grow up and get married. It is a very big day for them, just as it is for you. Therefore you should start the discussion on what they will wear early on. It is a great idea to make sure that they have new designer outfits if possible, so that they really have something special for the occasion. After all, it is hoped that you will only get married once. This means that they only have one chance to get dressed up in their finery for your wedding.

It is traditional for the fathers to wear suits, usually something similar to what the groom and groomsmen are wearing. In other words, if you have top hats and handkerchiefs, so should the parents. For the mothers, normally they will wear a dress. The usual fashion is a formal dress reaching down to around calf length, paired with a small jacket that covers the shoulders and the top of the dress. A hat or fascinator is usually provided for the hair as well, in the same color and preferably the same fabric. This gives you the perfect look for the mother of the bride and the mother of the groom. Generally speaking, they can break with tradition a little bit as well. For example, one of the mothers may wish to wear a suit rather than a dress. In this case, they can make the look less severe by choosing pastel colors.

Dress Shopping Tips

Now let's talk about some tips which will help when you are shopping for your dress. The process of finding your ideal dress can actually be quite stressful, mostly because this is one of the most important parts of the wedding. There is so much pressure to get it right, that it can at times be overwhelming. The first thing we have to say to you is to limit your entourage. If you have half the wedding party with you while you try and choose your dress, there will be too many conflicting opinions. Just one or two people should help you to search. If you have more with you, not only will you be taking up too much room in the shop, but you also may feel pressured into buying something that you do not want.

You should also watch your budget very carefully, as there may be small hidden costs to take into consideration. Find out how much it will cost to have any adjustments made, as these could eat into your budget considerably. You will need your veil or headpiece to come out of the same budget as well, so do not forget that. Do not stress out too much about the accessories and other clothing that you will wear with your gown at first. You can bring them to your final fitting appointment to make sure that everything works. You do not even need to bring your specific underwear with you on the first fitting. Most bridal shops will even have different types of bras available in the sitting room for you to try with the dress.

If you have fallen in love with a particular style that you have seen online, it is worth phoning ahead to your salon to make sure they have it in stock. If they do not, they should be able to arrange for it to be there when you come down. If you do not find what you want on your first trip, do not be too disappointed. You will find the right dress – it may just take a little more time than you expected.

It is also a really bad idea to try shopping as though you are going to lose weight or put it on. At the end of the day, it is almost impossible to predict what your body will be like by the time of the wedding, even if you have the best intentions. If you go for a dress which is far too small, and then do not lose the weight, the alterations will be costly. Just plan for what you have – it is the safest option. If you are not happy with your body now, lose weight before you try on your dress. Sample sales can help you to save money, but be aware that the first day of the sales is normally quite hectic. Go down on a later date to see what is available. This will save you some stress.

Attire Etiquette

There are a few more things still to iron out when it comes to attire. Of course, the wedding parties are not the only ones who need to consider what they are going to wear. There are also the guests, and if you wish them to wear something specific, you may need to let them know. The same is true if there are any colors or styles you wish them to stay away from. Give them plenty of notice if this is the case, so that they can do their shopping in preparation before the event.

The first matter of etiquette that you have to decide on is who pays for what. This is something that can follow tradition if you wish. It can certainly be much easier to decide things if you just go by tradition. This avoids arguments and prevents any bad feeling on either side. On the other hand, your particular situation may call for a break from tradition. This is something that you should discuss between yourselves. You can go with whatever feels right to you.

The next matter of etiquette is related to who wears what. As we have already seen, it is important that everyone sticks to the theme and color scheme. If you have one person in the wedding party who stands out, things will not look great. If you have a stubborn person who is refusing to wear what you have asked, then you need to seriously ask them to consider the situation. If they are not willing to change their mind for the biggest day of your life, perhaps they should not be part of your wedding ceremony. It may sound harsh, but they will surely come round to your way of thinking when you explain it this way.

As for the guests, it is important that they match your theme as well. Some people may feel uncomfortable asking the guests to stick to a certain theme, but it is your right to do so. After all, this is your wedding ceremony, and everyone who you have invited is there as your guest. If your theme calls for everyone to be wearing black and white, then state on the invites that they must wear black and white. The same goes for if you would like them to dress up, or if formal wear would be preferred. As your guests, they are the ones who should try to suit your theme, as it is your wishes they must follow. It is perfectly acceptable to ask them to dress according to your wishes.

Try to make it clear if there are any no nos that you wish to avoid as well. Some people may not realize that it is a faux pas to wear white unless you are requested to, because of the fact that it clashes with the bride. If that would make you uncomfortable, you can always send a message out to everyone that they must avoid the color with their invites.

The To-Do List

Now that we have considered all of the elements of attire that you need to think about, it is time to make a to-do list so that you can stay organized and on track. This will help you to achieve everything that you need before the big day. It is essential that you are able to get everything done on the right schedule and at the right time, so that nothing gets left out. Use the list below to help you decide what order things should be done in and what you need to tick off.

First phase: Deciding on Themes and Looks

Here is where you start to think about the overall theme of your wedding. Once you have chosen colors at the very least, you can start to get organized. The bride can look at images of wedding dresses online to get an idea of the kind of wedding dress she wants. She can also book into a wedding salon in order to start trying dresses on as well. The groom can also start thinking about his suit and what kind of accessories he would like. At the same time, you can consider the accessories and colors that your wedding party should wear.

Second phase: Choosing Outfits and Buying

Now is the time to start actually picking out the outfits and buying them. You can find your perfect wedding dress and order it, as well as having your first fitting. You can try on bridesmaids' dresses and purchase a set for your full party. The same can be done for accessories such as shoes, bags, jewelry, and so forth. The groomsmen and the groom can try on their suits for the first time and order them from the tailor. This is where you really start to see everything falling into place. You will also get a better idea of how much of your budget you have used by the time you have finished with this phase.

Third phase: Making Adjustments and Reviewing Changes

Once everything has been purchased, you need to make sure that it all fits as planned. The bride and groom should try on their wedding clothes and get them adjusted if necessary. If it was not possible to find bridesmaids' dresses that would fit everyone, now is also the time to make changes. The same is the case for suits for the groomsmen. By the end of this phase, everyone should be looking their best ready for the wedding.

Final phase: Last Minute Checks

Right before the ceremony, around a week before, you should make final adjustments. This means trying on everything and making sure it still fits. You may have lost weight through the stress of planning, or put it on from trying too many cakes. Younger members of the wedding party may have grown taller. If anyone is pregnant, they may have grown in an unexpected way. Do not wait until the day of the wedding to find out that something does not fit.

FLOWERS

Flowers: will highlight the wedding

Flowers are such an important part of your wedding day, from start to finish, that you will want to begin researching and planning exactly what you want early on. Don't make the mistake of leaving these choices until last, or believing that the floral arrangements, outside of the bridal bouquets, don't play a large part in the wedding. They do.

Besides offering a lovely effect for your guests, the flowers will highlight the wedding pictures, as well as those taken at the reception. You may want to go with floral arrangements that are true to the season you have chosen for the wedding. If the ceremony takes place in autumn, you may want to choose flowers in warm, spicy colors, such as burgundy, orange, and chocolate. For summer, try some cheerful daisies with sunflower centerpieces.

Typically, wedding flowers include at least bridal party bouquets, boutonnieres for the groom and groomsmen, decorations for the ceremony and reception, and, most importantly, the bride's bouquet. Some ladies like to include flowers, such as small bouquets or corsages, for the mothers of the bride and groom, and others prefer to have some type of floral accent for every person involved in the ceremony.

Choose your budget before retaining a florist. A good rule of thumb is to spend 8-10 percent of the overall wedding budget on the flowers.

Perhaps the color choice is the first decision to be made. You'll want to have your general wedding color choice firmly in place before you begin this journey. Then you can decide which way you want to go with decorations. Do you want flowers that match your wedding colors, or will you choose an accent color to highlight your wedding palette?

Secondly, what type of flowers do you prefer? Have you always dreamed of elegant yellow roses in your bouquet, or are you more of a fresh white daisy fan? Do you want small bouquets of sweet rounded perfection, or romantically flowing flowers spilling from your arms?

Online research will go a long way in helping you ascertain which types of floral arrangements fit in best with your designs. Getting advice from recently married friends can be a tremendous help, as well. These ladies can offer ideas for staying on budget, and share tips on what worked for them, and what did not.

Pinterest is a terrific site for searching a large variety of styles and finding exactly what you want for your own ceremony. Whether you are doing the flowers yourself, or choosing a florist, Pinterest will help you find ideas from classic elegance to fun and unique.

Once you have a good idea on the style and colors you prefer, it's time to find a florist. Keep an open mind while explaining your vision. Florists are experienced at taking a dream and turning it into a reality. Allow them to help you set your style, but stay true to your vision. It's your wedding, after all.

How to Choose a Florist

So it's time to choose your wedding florist. It's important to begin researching early on, but before you make your final decision, there are a few things that should have already been set in place.

Do you want a florist or a floral designer? A florist will work with you to expertly create lovely bouquets, boutonnieres, corsages, centerpieces, and the like. A floral designer will do all this, plus work the flowers into the entire wedding theme, coordinating centerpieces with napkins, table covers, and more.

Have your wedding date set. The florist will need to know the season in which you'll be married to make appropriate suggestions. Going with seasonal blooms can be less expensive, as well as adding to the theme of your wedding. Don't forget to consider seasonal berries, leaves, and the like to give your décor a truly unique design.

Have your venues chosen. Will your wedding be inside or outdoors? Is it a small area or a large one? This is important information that you'll want to share with your chosen florist.

Choose your wedding colors, and decide if you prefer to have flowers in corresponding colors, in accent colors, or perhaps a combination of both.

Know your budget. You don't want to get excited and plan flowers for the wedding of your dreams only to learn your budget will not allow such extravagance.

Does your wedding have a particular theme? This can be something as simple as a specific color or flower, butterflies, or the use of glimmering glitter within the floral arrangements, which adds a deeper dimension to the décor as the light shines on them. The theme can be as intricate as an evening in Paris or a princess ball. Use your imagination and find something that will be meaningful to you and fun for your guests.

Meet with a minimum of three florists before making the final decision. Take color swatches of the bridesmaid dresses, photos from the internet or magazines showing floral styles you like, and a photo of the wedding dress. Having a visual of these key items will help the florist make better choices. Bring a list of the total members in the entire wedding party, from bridesmaids and groomsmen all the way down to the flower girl and ring bearer. If you have a preliminary estimate of the number of wedding guests you expect, this can come in handy as well.

Take a notebook or tablet with you on the florist interviews so you can make notes on how you feel about the florist as well as their ideas. Notate the good points from the meeting, especially if a particular style or design is mentioned that you absolutely love.

After sharing your own ideas, keep an open mind while listening to suggestions from the florist. Ultimately the decision is your own, but consulting a professional and taking those ideas into consideration may take your dream from good to absolutely amazing.

Reception Flowers

Much like the bride is the centerpiece of the wedding ceremony, the table centerpieces are the stars of the reception hall. Your table décor is what will add beauty and intimacy to the blank canvas of the reception hall.

Reception flowers are not as simple as they seem. There are so many additions that can be joined with flowers to create gorgeous reception décor. Softly glowing candles in the midst of a lovely floral arrangement will add a romantic atmosphere, while highlighting the colors in the blooms themselves, especially when coupled with lower lighting. Adding gems inside a clear vase will create even more of a lovely glow, enhancing the light of the candles.

Consider a small, clear bowl of water with floating candles spaced in between the floral centerpieces. Or instead of larger flowers, have rings of flowers fashioned to fit around the glass bowls for a lovely mixture of light and color.

Try to stay away from tall flowers that will obstruct the view of guests as they try to converse with one another, or as they are watching the wedding festivities. Perhaps a different idea would be a long runner of short flowers down the center of the tables. For a Christmas wedding, try a bed of evergreen decorated with holly berries, poinsettias, small candles, and opalescent glitter to embody snow.

An arbor filled with flowers at the side of the dance floor will give the area a garden feel, as well as providing a lovely backdrop for the photographer, as well as guests, to take pictures.

Outside of the obvious centerpieces, there are less considered areas that you may want to trim with flowers as well. The cake table, for instance, could benefit from some well-placed blooms. The gift table should have at least one centerpiece, or perhaps a better idea might be swag of interwoven flowers trimmed along the edge of the table so there is plenty of room for wedding gifts.

The table where the wedding party will be seated absolutely must have lovely blooms to grace the table. Depending on your preference, these flowers can be the same as the centerpieces on the tables for your guests, or something a bit more exquisite.

If you want your beautiful wedding décor to spill out into every part of the reception, consider a vase or two of flowers for the restrooms at the venue. This will be a nice surprise, and lend an elegance to the affair.

Centerpieces are not the only factor that goes into designing the table décor. You will want to pick table coverings, napkins, dishes, and flat wear that will complement the colors and style of the flowers. No matter how outstanding your floral centerpieces are, if they are paired with old tablecloths, or with a clashing color, the desired effect will be completely ruined. Be sure to coordinate everything on the table together for the finest results.

Flowers for the Bride and Attendants

Choosing flowers for the bride, bridesmaids, and maid (or matron) of honor can be one of the most enjoyable of the wedding preparations. Have an informal meeting at your house or a local coffee shop with the bridal party and check out the many flower choices available in magazines and on websites. Take notes or bookmark pages where your favorite styles are found.

If you choose to include the opinions of your bridal party in the flower choices, being together in close proximity will make it easier to come to a decision about bridesmaid bouquets and corsages, as you will be able to brainstorm together.

There are many ways of going about choosing the design for these floral arrangements. You may want all the bouquets to be exactly the same. Perhaps you prefer they all include the wedding colors, but want each bouquet to feature different flowers. On the flip side, you might like to create bouquets that have the same flower, but each in a different color. You may want to allow your bridal party to choose their favorite flower for each bouquet, as long as it is in line with your color palette. It's your wedding, and, like Burger King, you can have it your way.

Of course, the bride's bouquet is often the largest and most elaborately designed. She is the ultimate centerpiece of the day, after all, and deserves to shine above the rest. Some brides like to use white flowers with large blooms, and accent these with smaller flowers in the wedding colors.

166

Something that should never be overlooked is how the colors of the bouquets mesh with the color of the dress. Of course this is not such an issue for a bride who is wearing white or cream, but you want to make certain that the bouquets go well with the bridal party dresses. Conflicting color choices will not only take away from the beauty of the ceremony, but will mar those beautiful wedding pictures that you will be showing people for years to come.

Bouquets may be made simply of one type of flower or several. Many brides like to adorn the bouquet with ribbons, glitter, lace, or other unique stamps of her personality. Small fillers such as baby's breath add a sweet touch to bolder floral, softening the overall look.

Don't be afraid to take unusual ideas to your florist. A vision does not need to be popular to be amazing. You never know, you might start a new trend! If you've chosen a professional florist, share your thoughts with her, and she will steer you in the right direction. Again, this is your day, and ultimately you should have what you desire.

Flowers for the Groom and Attendants

We do not often relate flowers to gentlemen, so what exactly are boutonnieres, and what are their purposes?

Boutonnieres are typically a small flower or tiny floral arrangement that is worn in the lapel buttonhole of a tuxedo.

These are worn by the groom, best man, groomsmen, ushers, and ring bearer.

It is a nice gesture to include male family members in this tradition, which will go a long way to making them feel included in the festivities, as well as identify them as belonging to the family of the special couple. It is appropriate to gift boutonnieres to the fathers, uncles, grandfathers, and any other close relationships you want to include.

The tradition of wearing a boutonniere is really quite sweet, as the groom wears the arrangement on his left lapel, closest to his heart.

As with bride and bridesmaid bouquets, there are many options available when choosing the boutonnieres for the groom and groomsmen. Very often the boutonniere is made of one bloom or bud, maybe with some small accent as a leaf or baby's breath. It can also be done with several small flowers or buds.

There are a great variety of color choices, as well. Perhaps you'd like the groom's boutonniere to match the bride's bouquet, the best man's boutonniere to match the maid of honor's bouquet, and so on.

The groom's arrangement can consist of one of the wedding colors, and the groomsmen can take the remaining color or colors. Use your own creativity here to design exactly what you desire. Don't go with tradition simply for tradition's sake. A boutonniere consisting of a single white carnation may be a classic choice for one bride, but a monumental bore for another. If bright colors are your preference, then go with bright colors. There's no right or wrong answer here. You have full sway over your wedding details. Although, at least in this decision, if not in others, be sure to get the groom's input, if he has any.

Astroemeria, also called the Peruvian lily or lily of the Incas, seems to be a fairly popular choice for wedding boutonnieres. The blooms are gorgeous and come in a large variety of colors, but before choosing this flower, do some research on the plant. The sap of the Peruvian lily can be harmful if it enters a person's blood stream, and if you are using corsages or boutonnieres with pins, or even scratchy accents, the sap could leak through a small scratch or wound caused by the boutonniere.

If your groom is simply not interested in wearing flowers, despite your best efforts, then a nice alternative is a pocket square. Like the boutonniere, the pocket square goes on the left side of the tuxedo. It is a small handkerchief that is tucked in the left pocket. The colors can match the dresses or bouquets of the bride and bridesmaids.

Your florist will help you make choices based on your preferences. Have fun with the floral details. Relax and enjoy shopping through the exquisite blooms that come in hues too numerous to mention. Flowers are beautiful. This should not just be another wedding chore. It should be a delightful stroll through a garden of your choosing.

Flowers for Children

Having children in your wedding party can be a fun and whimsical addition to your wedding. Though they may cause some commotion and have difficulty following through and remembering their duties, children bring light and love into a wedding ceremony. After all, isn't that what a wedding is all about?

Flower girls and ring bearers should be between the ages of 3 and 7. Junior bridesmaids are generally 12 to 16. Young men who are too old to be ring bearers are simply groomsmen, like their older counterparts.

However, these rules are not set in stone, and you should feel the freedom to plug your young loved ones into your wedding as you see fit.

If you have more little ones you would like to include, there are other roles beyond the flower girl and ring bearer. Children can add a great deal to a wedding ceremony by carrying candles, handing out programs (if you have them), attending the guest book, or handing out bubbles, rice, or birdseed after the wedding to toss at the bride and groom.

Flowers for the children can be an echo of the older members of the wedding party, or they can be completely different. The flower girl will obviously be carrying a basket with petals inside to scatter along the aisle as she walks. Therefore, a small bouquet would be too awkward for her to handle. She can still be adorned with lovely flowers, though. The hair is a favorite area to showcase beautiful blooms on little girls. A ring of flowers to be worn on the head, a headband encased in flowers, or just a simple bloom tucked into the flower girl's hair will make her feel special, and add pizzazz to her wedding finery.

Of course, if you prefer not to have flower petals strewn along the walkway, then a tiny bouquet would certainly be appropriate for the flower girl.

The ring bearer can wear a tiny boutonniere or pocket square, depending on your preference.

The junior bridesmaids definitely need bouquets in a smaller version of those the bridesmaids will carry. Again, they can match with the bridesmaids, or be a creation unique to the younger bridesmaids.

The important thing to remember when choosing flowers for the younger wedding party participants is not to go overboard. A tiny girl will look silly carrying a heavy bouquet, and she will tire easily, as well. Some of those floral arrangements can be heavy! Choose a smaller arrangement that will not overwhelm the little girls.

To-Do List

You may be surprised by how many flowers you might need for your wedding. Prior to meeting with your chosen florist, it is a good idea to write a checklist with all the categories of flowers and floral arrangements you will need.

If you are not sure exactly what you will need outside of bouquets and boutonnieres, online research can be helpful. If you have friends who have recently married, ask for their help in making your list. There could be many categories that you simply don't think about because you don't have experience planning a wedding. Don't fret, though, even if you don't have outside help, your florist will be of huge assistance.

The following information should help you ascertain which types of floral arrangement you will need, so when you meet with the florist, you have at least an idea of how many categories in your wedding will require flowers or floral arrangements.

For the wedding party, you will need bouquets for the bride, bridesmaids, and junior brides. The flower girl will need either a basket of petals or a small bouquet. Any floral accents such as ring of flowers or headband for the ladies to wear in their hair should be included as well.

The groom, groomsmen, ring bearer, officiant, ushers, and chosen family members will receive boutonnieres.

Corsages or small nosegays can be gifted to the ladies in the family, such as mothers, grandmothers, aunts, sisters, or other women close to the bride and groom.

Some areas to think about decorating for the ceremony include the entryway, pews or chairs, welcome table, and the altar.

Reception flowers may take the most thought, and what you will need really depends on your reception venue. If the place you are holding the reception is already a gorgeous masterpiece, then you may not need to decorate as much, and simply allow the natural beauty to shine.

If you feel your reception hall needs a lot of floral décor, you might want to consider the following areas. Obviously, the wedding party table and those at which the guests will be eating need to be filled with lovely flowers. However large or small you want your flowers to be is up to you, but it's important to add flowers to the tables to create a more romantic, exciting atmosphere.

Some less thought of areas that some brides like to enhance are the cake table, the gift table, the bar (if you have one), and even the restroom. The latter suggestion is a nice touch in completing the flow of your décor all the way throughout the venue.

You may want to offer an area where your photographer, and your wedding guests, can take photos to commemorate the occasion. Floral arrangements always make a lovely backdrop no matter if you are taking romantic couple photos or cute pictures of the children in your wedding. This will also give something back to all the wedding guests who have taken the time to shop for you and gift you with lovely presents or the always welcome cash.

There is no doubt that flowers add a special touch to weddings, no matter what the theme. Whether small and dainty or large and wild, flowers add the finishing touch to a day that is worth remembering.

PLANNING YOUR WEDDING RECEPTION

The Wedding Reception

The wedding reception is likely to be the most important and memorable party you will ever plan. It is also likely to take up the largest amount of the budget. Because of this, it is essential that you make the right investments and also plan this part of the wedding very carefully. It is also the case that the largest number of guests will be coming to your reception, while the ceremony itself will have a small number of guests attending. This means that if you want to impress anyone or create lasting memories, the reception will be the time to do it.

There is a lot to think about, so it is recommended that you start to plan everything as soon as possible. You will of course have decided on your theme, which means that you will have an idea of how you want the reception to look. You will also be able to decide on a location fairly easily if you have an idea of the sense or theme that you wish to impart. For example, a classic styled or grand wedding might require a country house or manor as the setting. If you are trying to give an impression of the intimacy of your relationship, you might hold the reception in the pub where you first met. You can see how the ideas grow based on the way you want your wedding to be.

The reception is also where you have to think about things like seating plans and guest arrangements. You will be likely to add the wider sides of both of your families, as well as all of your friends and any work colleagues who are appropriate to invite. You are likely to have some people at the reception that one or the other of you does not know. This is because the reception is a place for anyone who has any impact on your life to come. It is also important in some situations to invite those who should be there for political reasons. For example, you might invite your boss because it may increase your chances of promotion. You may invite your second cousin, whom you have not seen in 10 years, simply because inviting family is the right thing to do.

There are plenty of minefields to navigate in this part of the planning phase. You have to make sure that everything is done correctly, organized, paid for out of your wedding budget, and so forth before the wedding date. It can be a lot of work, and this is probably the stage where people most often feel that they need help. Having a wedding planner will certainly make things easier for you, as we have discussed before, but you can also sort things out yourself so long as you have the time to do it. Set aside the biggest part of your planning time for anything to do with the reception. You will certainly need it, as you are about to discover.

The Site of Your Reception

Here is where you really need to book in advance. Most people will think about booking their reception venue very soon after they become engaged. The reason is that many of the best venues can be booked up to a year in advance, or even further. If you wish to get married in the place of your dreams, then you need to think about it sooner, rather than later. You may even find that you end up scheduling the wedding itself based on the date that your venue is available. Start looking immediately – you may not be able to decide on a venue for a while, so putting it off will certainly not work in your favor.

There are plenty of factors to think about when you are deciding on your venue. First of all, you need enough space in the venue to accommodate all of the guests that you have invited, or are intending to invite. You need a space where everyone can sit and eat, a space for the food to be laid out, and a place for dancing later on. Not everyone will want to dance at the same time, so it is not plausible to be able to take away all of the tables and chairs. You need to have at least some of them left later on in the evening.

The venue should also be in an area which will be accessible for all of your guests. If it is difficult to reach, or does not have much space available for parking, you may wish to consider hiring a coach to bring everyone to the venue. This may cause an awkward situation when everyone wants to leave later. You can either pay for them to have taxis, or make other arrangements so that they are able to leave at the time of their choosing. If all of this seems like too much hassle, then you understand why you must choose a place that is easy to get to and has ample parking.

Budget is also one of the biggest considerations that you have to keep in mind. If you cannot afford the place, then you simply cannot have it. You can always try to haggle with the owners of the venue, and see if they have any wiggle room, but it is not likely to be the case. You may suddenly be able to arrange a discount if you are booking a last-minute date, but as we have already discussed, this is not an advisable strategy. You may end up simply not being able to get married on the date that you have chosen! Remember that you need to book a reception venue early on so that you can send out invitations to all of your guests. They need to know where they will be going; otherwise the day itself will be chaos. If you do not wish to spend your wedding day chasing after your guests, you need to arrange it in advance.

Seating

Seating is one of the most stressful things that you have to organize for the whole wedding. Unfortunately, you have to decide where everyone is going to sit. This means that you have to navigate old family feuds, favoritism, and personality clashes with grace. Everyone must be seated in an appropriate place, with people that they may find interesting to talk to, and away from anyone with whom they might have a dispute. That sounds a lot easier than it is in practice, so if it sounds difficult, you understand how much of a nightmare it can be.

The solution is to face everything with a practical nature. Start off with the most problematic guests. Your parents and the wedding parties need to be seated at the highest tables, giving them a position of honor. After this, put in anyone who might need to sit next to someone else, or needs to be far away from someone else. Then you can fill in the gaps with everyone that you have left on your list. Do not worry too much about getting it absolutely perfect. It is unlikely that you will be able to achieve this, because there are so many permutations even with a small wedding that you will be pulling your hair out in despair. Just focus on getting a solution that will at least half please everybody. This may well be the best that you can do.

The way that you set up your seating arrangements largely depends on how many people you can fit at each table. You need to obtain this information from your venue as early as possible, so that you can start to arrange the details. You can feel free to set out the seating arrangements early on. However, as you get your RSVPs back, some of them may be from people who are unable to attend the reception. This means that you will be taking them out of the seating plan. If someone requests that they can bring a plus one with them, and you do not mind, then you will also need to fit another back into the chart.

When everything is arranged, and ready for the big night, you can think about presentation. Most people like to have a place card on the table which indicates the name of the person who should be sitting there. You can also have a chart displayed near the entrance of the reception venue, so that people can check where they should be sitting before they enter. This will take away some of the confusion early on. It will make things much easier, and will allow people to get to their tables without milling around too much. Presentation is very important, so make sure that the chart and the place cards all match your theme and colors. This will prevent anything from looking out of place. You can have your chart professionally made if you want to really make an impact.

Caterer

Food is a big part of the event, as you would not want people to go hungry. This means that you will have to provide some catering at your reception. If you want to make the event as inexpensive as possible, then you may possibly consider providing some elements of the catering yourself, as we have already discussed. This is something that is very difficult to organize, however, and you will be better off getting it all taken care of by a professional team. Normally a catering company will provide not only the food, but also plates and cutlery, any sauces needed, and even serving staff to lay all of the food out.

You need to decide what type of wedding food you are going to have. Realistically, there are only two options. The first is a sit down meal, where everyone orders their choice of food before the day and it is served in several courses. This allows everyone to eat a full meal, but is usually only reserved for very expensive and formal affairs. What is normally held to be the usual way of doing things is to hold a buffet. This entails laying out all of the food on a series of tables, normally in an area away from the seating, with plates and cutlery available nearby. Then your guests can queue up and walk along with their plates, picking up any food which appeals to them. They can go up as many times as they like, and you can also have a dessert table to finish things off.

Either way, you need to organize your caterers, and tell them what you are looking for. You can organize your own menu based on the kinds of foods that you would like to have. Doubtless, they will also have a list of the common items which people choose, so that you can decide more easily. You have to remember to cater for all of the guests that you have invited. This means keeping track of what dietary requirements everyone has. If you have vegetarian or vegan attendees, then food which is suitable for them must be kept away from meat or dairy products which might cause some contamination. If you have people with halal requirements, then you should also set aside some food for them. Gluten free diets must also be observed, and so on and so forth.

You also need to be aware of allergies. There are some people who are so allergic to nuts that they will swell up if they are in the same room as them. This means keeping nuts off the menu and out of the area if you have someone who would be affected in this way. Ask for people to RSVP with their allergies if they have any. This will give you an idea of what to avoid, and you can pass this information on to your caterers to make sure everything will be safe.

Foods: Planning the Menu

Of course, once you have figured out what everyone cannot eat, you still need to think about what they actually can eat. You need to plan your menu. There is a lot to take into consideration here. You need an overall theme for your food (and this could even be simply traditional wedding food or a traditional buffet). You need to figure out how much food you will need for all of your guests. You also need to figure out how the courses will be laid out. Do you bring out appetizers, then more substantial food, and then a dessert? Or do you just lay it all out along the buffet tables and let your guests pick and choose what they like?

There are certainly plenty of ways to decide. You can think about your wedding theme and what may match it, for example. If you want everyone to dress up like characters from Doctor Who while the groom dresses as one of the doctors and the bride as a companion, then the choice of food can be simple. Have everything themed around something from the show, and even look through old episodes to see if they ever ate specific things. This can be a fun part of the theme, and while it is good not to go overboard by sacrificing quality for theme, it can add substantially to the atmosphere of the reception.

You can also decide based on culture. Let's say that you are a woman with Indian parents, getting married to a man with a Jewish heritage. You can have foods in your buffet which are traditionally used in each of these cultures. If you both share the same culture, then laying out the choices can be even easier. Just make sure that you have enough variety. If there are not enough traditional foods to draw from, then add some of your favorites as well.

You can just go with favorites from the outset if you are not too worried about a theme for you food. Pick the things that you like to eat. You can be courteous to the wedding party and add some of their favorites as well. If your sister has always loved eating breadsticks, then you can have a variety of different flavors available. They can sit on the table next to your favorite sandwiches, your spouse's preferred fruits, and the favorite dessert of the best man. This can make sure that everyone has something they enjoy on the table, even if it makes it seem a little disjointed.

Just make sure that everything is suitable for a buffet format. Normally you will want the majority of the options to be finger food. These can be picked up, put on a plate, and then eaten with very little hassle. If you have soups, curries, pasta dishes, or similar options, you may wish to provide bowls and spoons. This will prevent messes on the wedding clothes of you and your guests.

Drinks

Drinks are a very important part of the reception, too. Even if you were to declare that you were having no alcohol at your reception, perhaps because of religious reasons, you still need to think about drinks. If you do not provide them, then you will have a lot of thirsty guests by the end of the night!

It is up to you how you deal with this area of the wedding, however. If your venue has bar facilities, then they may wish to charge for all drinks which are ordered by your guests. You can either put some money behind the bar to cover this, or ask your guests to cover their own drinks.

One thing that you should normally have on hand, so long as you are going to allow alcohol, is champagne. There should be a few bottles, at least, to go around for all of your guests for the traditional toast during the speeches. If you do not have the budget to cover nice champagne all night long, you can always switch to wine or other spirits after the speeches have been done. You can even go for a lower cost sparkling wine if you wish. Many people will not be able to tell the difference, or will not mind.

You should make sure that there is a plentiful supply of soft drinks as well. You can have a jug of water placed in the center of each table so that your guests can help themselves whenever they like. Tap water is fine, and you can add some ice, if you want, to keep it fresh. A slice of lemon or lime placed in the jug can also make it more appealing. Options such as orange juice, other fruit juices, and perhaps lemonade or cola should also be available. This will suit the tastes of all of your guests.

You may also want to check with the bar beforehand about what their prices will be. In some cases, you will find that the prices are put up to coincide with a wedding, as they know that you or your guests will want to buy something. If this is the case, there is another alternative to consider. If the venue will allow it, you may be able to bring in your own drinks, rather than sticking to theirs. This can save you some money, if you are able to get to wholesalers or have some contributions from guests.

Above all, make sure that you have this area covered before everything else is settled. If you need to put more of an investment into drinks, then you need to know about it early on so that you can adjust your budget. Do not just assume that a fully catered venue includes drinks in their price. Get it in writing – or plan to provide your own drinks. This is incredibly important as it can be something that drives budgets up by a huge amount.

Wedding Cake

Everyone knows that the wedding cake is one of the biggest parts of the reception. It is traditional to have a photograph of the two of you cutting the cake together, both with one hand on the knife. This is another part of the symbolism of the joining together of the two of you in marriage. But what is important is what your wedding cake looks, and tastes like. Just as with the dress, it can be a decision which rests largely on style and taste. Just like the wedding dress, it is also something that people will be talking about for a long time to come if you get it right.

There are a lot of different options that you can consider when it comes to your wedding cake. There is no one style which has to be used and the world is pretty much your oyster when it comes to design inspiration. You can have any arrangement that you like. If you keep up with the latest fashions, you will notice that some types of cake are more popular at certain times. For example, there has recently been a lot of talk about the use of cupcakes. Having a large amount of these miniature cakes instead of just one single solid cake makes a real statement. However, even that fashion is starting to become less popular now, mainly because so many people have already done it. You can browse wedding websites and magazines in order to get an idea of what the current fashion is at any given time.

You do not have to abide by fashion though. You are free to choose whatever appeals to you the most. Generally speaking, most people will have one large and well decorated cake, which stands as the center piece and is the one that you cut for your photographs. You may then have a number of smaller or less decorated cakes which may be distributed among your guests, if you have a large number of people attending. This will save on having to have a fancy cake which is large enough to include everyone, which could be quite expensive and time-consuming. Remember that everyone at the reception would expect to have a piece of the cake. It is not appropriate to leave anyone without.

Traditionally, the cake would stand on several tiers, each one wider than the one above it. At the very top of the cake you will have a bride and groom cake topper. This is made either from sugar or from plastic, and stands as a representation of you and your husband as you enter married life. Many people have a lot of fun with the cake toppers. They can be humorous, they can be caricatures, or they can depict you doing something other than standing around in your wedding clothes. Another fun thing to do is to have one made which realistically depicts both of you. You can have this done even down to the details of the dress.

Music

Last but not least, you also have to think about the music that you will have at your reception. It is very important that you are able to choose something which fits the occasion. It should also represent both of your personalities, and complement your taste in music. But that does not mean that you should alienate other people. For example, if the two of you are very much into metal music, then by all means have a playlist full of metal music. But have some hits from the current charts, and some golden oldies, as well. This will allow everyone to get up and dance even if they do not share your tastes.

The music is played during the evening when it is time for people to get up, dance, and have a good time. You do not necessarily have to start it at a certain time, though it is normally accepted that it should be played when the buffet is over. You can also have it playing during the buffet if you want to encourage people to come and go as they please. It is all up to you how you want to do things.

You can also decide your own preferred direction when it comes to the choice of having a DJ, simply playing some CDs or an iPod, or having a live band. There are positive and negative sides to all of these options. Having a live band may be more expensive, but it is likely to be more impressive, and make the evening more of a memorable one. Especially if you are a fan and can get a band that you love. It could prove to be a really fantastic occasion. Otherwise, having a live DJ will provide the live entertainment without costing you as much. A DJ is also a great idea because they can adapt to the current mood of the party, allowing them to play whatever they like whenever it seems suitable and even taking requests.

The most important thing of all is to make sure that you have chosen your first dance. This is the moment when you and your new spouse dance together, under the eyes of all of your guests. You should pick a song which means something to you, either because of the romantic lyrics or because it reflects a particular time in your relationship. You can slow dance to it, or train yourself in a more adventurous style of dance if you are feeling up to it. Remember to get plenty of practice in before the wedding so that you are not nervous on the day itself. As your song continues to play, other people will begin to take part in the dance, taking to the dance floor so that you are no longer alone. That is when the party will really begin. Everyone can party late into the night when there is music playing for them to enjoy.

To-Do List

When you look at all of the elements that need to be under control in order to create the ideal reception, you will realize that there is a lot to think about. Because of this, we are able to create a to-do list for you here which you can simply check off as you go along. Make a list of these things somewhere in your wedding planning notes, and go through them one by one until you are sure that everything is done. That way, you will know that your reception is on course to be a great one.

The first thing to do is to find a venue and book it. This means that you must schedule in some time to view venues, and also decide upon a budget for it. Have an idea of what date you want to choose before you start looking at venues. Finally, decide on the venue that you prefer, and make the booking. Now that you have done this, you can start to think about a caterer.

First, decide on what type of catering you would like. It may help to get some preliminary quotes at this stage from catering companies who can provide different forms of catering. Make a choice about how much food you would like, what type of food you need, and how it will be served. Of course, you need to have your guest list sorted out before you can be sure of this. Then you can provide a fully itemized and clear menu to your catering service. They will be able to give you a final quote and you can sign contracts.

Along with the menu, it is time to think about the drinks. Discuss drink services with your venue, and find out what they offer. Ask them what you are allowed to do or not allowed to do. Then you can make a decision, and put everything in so that it will be ready for the night.

Look at the seating plan and think about who needs to sit where. This stage is likely to take longer than you would even think possible, so set aside plenty of time for it. Work on your plan until you are sure that you have got it right.

Next, you can look at invitations, and perhaps get some quotes from design companies or printers who will be able to make what you want.

After this, you seriously need to get started on choosing your wedding cake. Plenty of bakeries will offer tasting sessions where you can try the different types of wedding cake they make. They will also show you the decorations that are possible, so that you can come away from the session with a clear idea of what you want.

Lastly, look at booking the entertainment. Do not leave this too long just in case the entertainment that you have had your heart set on becomes booked.

WEEDING & GIFT REGISTRY

Your Guide to A Perfect Wedding Registry

Your wedding will not be complete without having your wedding registry. It is one of the few occasions where you can actually pick the gifts that you want to receive. As a couple, it would be fun to register your gifts and let your guests know your wish list so you can actually receive items that you really would love to have in your new home.

Wedding Registry Basics

Wedding registry or bridal registry is your list of items that you wish to receive as wedding gifts from a particular business establishment, be it an online or a physical store. The list of items is given to your guests so they can choose the items to purchase for you as a gift. Your preferred merchant then keeps tabs of the items that are already purchased and those that are still available. It makes gift selection for your guests easier because the store would know the preference of the bride and groom. Although wedding registry can be a fun activity for wedding planning, it can also get overwhelming and stressful. Here are some guides in making a perfect wedding registry.

Starting your wedding registry

To start your wedding registry, you can choose to go to register at the physical store location or you can do online registration.

To start a registry at a physical store location, sign up at the customer service counter. After signing up, you will be given a list of items that are usually registered as wedding gifts from the store and a barcode scanner by the store attendant. You can roam around the store to find the items you would like to receive as gifts and scan them to add to your registry. You can always go back to the store to make adjustments or add items you might have missed even after you have finished your registry.

Registering in online bridal registry is almost the same as the doing it at a physical store. You need to sign in first at the wedding registry section on the website of your preferred merchants. Then you can browse the items from their list and select items for your registry. Once you finish your registry, you can still visit the online store to add items you like or to make adjustments.

Choosing where to register

It is not enough that you just sign up for a wedding registry. It is essential also that you also pick the right stores to register. Here are tips that can help you make a better registry choice.

- Sign up at a national store with a good reputation so even guests that will be coming from out of town will have no difficulty in purchasing their gifts from your registry.
- Offer your guests an option to purchase from off-line and online stores because some of them may be too busy to shop at a physical store and will prefer to purchase the gift online.

- Register with two or three merchants to give your guests more options.
- Enroll at the commonly registered stores as they will have a wider variety of gift options for you and your guests to choose from.

Wedding Registry Etiquette that Every Couple Should Know

Creating your wedding registry is one fun pre-wedding activity for you and your significant others. But sometimes you can get lost on the process because of numerous choices that keeps piling up in front of you. To avoid being overwhelmed, couples should consider the following wedding registry etiquette to guide you.

Create your wedding registry early

Sign up for your wedding registry in advance to give you and your guests ample time to choose items as wedding gifts. It is ideal for you to create your registry four to six months in advance of your wedding day. This will not only give guests time to purchase gifts for your actual wedding, but also will give them ideas of what to give for your engagement and pre-wedding parties.

Create your registry together

Do create your wedding registry together. Remember that it is not just about the bride or the groom, but you as a couple. So it is expected that both of you will contribute to its creation. You are building a home that will last you a lifetime. It is sensible that both of you will love and enjoy the items that you are going to receive as wedding gifts.

Register for a lot of gift items

Register for enough gifts so that guests will have more options to choose from. It is better to register for twice the number of items than the number of your guests. Enlist gift items in a variety of prices and choose individual items rather than choosing sets. You must have a balance of expensive items and affordable ones.

Register with two or three stores

Do not limit your wedding registry to one store only. It is better to choose two or three national stores with lots of home basics to give your guests options on where to shop.

Do not include your wedding registry information in your invitation

It is unwise to include your wedding registry information in your wedding invitation. If you already have created your wedding registry, inform your immediate family members and close friends and let them inform other guests. On the other hand, it is fine for you to give your guests information of your wedding registry if you are asked directly by guests.

Do not ask for money outright

It is still consider a taboo to ask for money as wedding gifts. But if money is what you want to receive for your wedding, your family could be the one to communicate this delicate information to your guests. However, this should be done in subtle way. There are also some websites nowadays that let couples register for stocks or for their honeymoon to make monetary registry requests less uncomfortable.

Be gracious and write "thank you" notes

It is ideal for you to write thank you notes within six weeks after you receive the wedding gifts. In your thank you notes refer to the specific items that you received and include reasons why you loved receiving the gift. If you fall behind this timeline because of your busy wedding schedule, make an effort to send the thank you notes at the soonest time available. This will let your guests know that they are well appreciated.

The Wedding Registry Must Haves

When you sign up for your wedding registry, most stores will provide you a list of the traditional wedding registry items such as sets of fine china, flatware and glasses. While most couples still opt to follow the traditional wedding registry items, some now find this irrelevant to them. Thus, in building your registry list, it is better to choose items that are practical and that you will actually use, rather than sets and pieces that will only accumulate dust in your cabinets and cupboards. Here is a list of wedding registry essentials you must check out to complete your wish list.

White Dinnerware

All-white dinnerware is very versatile in your home. It is easy to dress up for special occasions or dress down for your daily use. It looks lovely when paired with colorful accent pieces on your table such as table napkins or colored glass. White is the best color to use in food presentation, thus even if you are only serving a simple meal it gives the impression of high class elegance.

If you are not a fan of an all-white place setting, you may opt for white dinnerware with accent colors. Look for plates that are durable, microwaveable and dishwasher safe.

Embellished Flatware

You may ask yourself why you want that fancy flatware. The reason is that embellished flatware adds interest to your table setting without going overboard. You can choose flatware that is rimmed in gold or with gilded designs. You can also opt for all silver flatware with interesting patterns. Choose dishwasher safe and sturdy pieces that could last you a lifetime.

Timeless China Set

Some couples may think that it is no longer relevant for them to get a china set as a wedding gift. But while you may not use it on a daily basis, you are sure to host one or two special occasions in your lifetime. Thus, having china set in a classic pattern is a must in your wedding registry. Look for patterns in stylish neutrals or metallic colors.

Cocktail Party Basics

Hosting an impromptu party with drinks for friends and family is inevitable in every couple's home. Hence, it is necessary that you stock up on your bar essentials. Bar glasses should be your top consideration, followed by a bar set that includes a shaker, jigger, bottle opener and tongs. Also include appetizer plates and cheese platters. You can also have some big items, such as bar carts, on your list.

Colored Glassware

Although clear glassware is a must have in your registry list, you can opt to include colored glassware to add spice and accent to your table. You may choose to include colored glassware to your bar essentials or to your everyday tumbler. Choose deep colors that will add pizzazz to your table, but will blend with your other glass pieces.

Hobby Items

You may also include hobby items that reflect your interests and passions as a couple in your gift registry. It can be anything from camping gear, power tools or a barbecue grill as long as you will actually use it.

Travel Essentials

It is also practical to include travel essentials to your wedding registry as you can actually use them whenever you need to go out of town. A sturdy suitcase with wheels and a nice carry-on bag are considered a wise investment for frequent travelers. It is important to consider the trips that you frequently take so you would know what kind of travel essentials you need most.

In the modern wedding registry, fun, practical items such as gadgets, electronics, backyard essentials and recreational items are mostly welcome to be included. Some couples may also opt to have a charity registry if they feel they already have the home essentials. Whatever you choose to include in your registry, bear in mind that these are the items that you don't only love to have but also will also be used in your home.

HONEYMOON

Honeymoon Planning

Your wedding was the most magical day of your life. It was a day full of fun, excitement, family, friends, and of course, loves. Likewise, your honeymoon will be the most magical trip of your life. Your honeymoon will be your first trip as Mr. and Mrs. It will be your first trip together as a married couple full of love, passion and a strong sense of adventure. However, if you don't take the necessary steps to plan your honeymoon – this magical trip can quickly turn into the most stressful trip of your lives. In order to avoid that outcome, here are a few tips to help you properly plan the honeymoon of your dreams.

First, the two of you need to decide on a location. Ask yourselves the following questions, then see the next sections for more information. Will you be traveling to romantic Hawaii or will you be staying somewhere more local? This decision will be heavily influenced by two external factors – budget and time. If you would like to travel a farther distance, than make sure the travel expense is within your budget and that you are both able to take enough time from work to get the most out of your trip. Additionally, when determining a location you should consider places that you both would like to see and activities that interest both of you. Going to Hawaii is an incredible trip, but if neither of you likes spending time on the beach and in the sun – it may not be a good fit.

Once you have selected a location you need to focus on what it is you would like to do. Will you be staying in one hotel for two weeks or will you be spending a few nights at several hotels? What sites are you interested in seeing? Where are these sites located in proximity to each other? Furthermore, are you sightseers or do you prefer to spend time in the spa or by the pool? Once you determine what it is that you like to do, you can plan the perfect trip.

Finally, book your trip. It is important to book the entire trip in advance. That is, make sure that you purchase your plane tickets, book your hotels and make reservations at the places you are planning on seeing. Try not to overbook yourselves. Often it will take you longer to get from one place to another than you think. If you overbook your trip, it can make it very stressful, as well as prevent the two of you from spending relaxing, quality time together. Lastly, don't be afraid to be spontaneous. Leave a day or two open to explore at your own pace. It is very common that you discover things at the location that you did not find on an internet search. Thus, it is important to give yourselves some leeway and to be open minded. Try new restaurants, new bars, ask the locals what they recommend and most importantly enjoy your time together as a married couple.

Types of Honeymoons

Honeymoons come in many "shapes and sizes", that is, they take on the characteristics which you give them. Honeymoons can be unique, or they can be generic. They can be incredibly elegant and expensive, or they can be simple and done on a budget. Moreover, honeymoons can be themed – city honeymoons, beach honeymoons, safari honeymoons – you name it, it can be done. So with all of these options, how do you choose? And what are the options available to you? We will list a few preparatory steps to help you decide and offer some fun suggestions.

First, as is true with any decision – you need to know what you and your spouse enjoy. If you hate the heat, a safari may not be the best option. Likewise if you don't enjoy the cold, skiing may not be your best choice either. Therefore, know what you enjoy doing as a couple – after all this vacation is "your vacation".

Next know your budget and availability. Don't plan a million dollar honeymoon if you do not have the budget for that. Likewise, don't look into three week honeymoons if you can only secure two weeks off from work. Keep this in mind when making your choice, as it will limit your decision (in a good way) and remove stress.

Now that you have a few steps to help you decide, we need to look at different types of honeymoons and what they can offer. As we mentioned above, each honeymoon is different. However, it is important to note, multiple people experience the same honeymoon destination in different ways – the entire experience is what you make of it. Here are a couple fun suggestions.

Beach Honeymoons

What could be more relaxing than sprawling out on the white, powdery sand of a gorgeous beach? Beach honeymoons are a popular option because they offer the relaxation couples need after planning their wedding. Beach honeymoons also offer a lot of diversity. Because you are close to the water, a beach honeymoon can offer fun activities like jet skiing, snorkeling, scuba diving and more. Depending on the location of the beach resort, there may be options for hiking and other fun adventures that you can share together as a new couple. At night, you can enjoy moon lit walks on the beach and of course enjoy the gourmet dinners. Often, beach resorts provide an active night life, filled with food, music, drinks, dancing and live performances.

City Honeymoons

If you are not the relaxation type of couple, or, if you enjoy relaxing in a different environment – then a city honeymoon might be a good choice. Booking a suite at a luxury city hotel can allow you to maximize your enjoyment of their amenities, while offering you the freedom to explore a new and exciting city. Take advantage of sleeping in, room service, the hot tub and all that your hotel has to offer – and just before you get cabin fever, feel free to book reservations at a gourmet restaurant or tickets to a live show. The city honeymoon is one of the most diverse options available – this is because city life provides so many entertainment options for so many different types of people.

Whether or Not you should Use a Travel Agent

Your honeymoon is a vacation of a lifetime – so it is important to plan it properly. Whenever one begins to plan a vacation, the question of whether or not to utilize the expertise of a travel agent is raised. There can be many benefits to hiring a travel agent. They can help you find good deals. They can give you advice that you otherwise would not be able to get. They can utilize their years of experience and contacts to help you book popular hotels and they can give great recommendations. On the other hand, travel agents can be very expensive. Furthermore, if the travel agent doesn't know you, they many not plan a trip exactly to your likes and interests as a couple. Therefore you are stuck in a quandary, which begs the question – should you hire a travel agent?

There are several considerations you should take into account when asking this question. These considerations range from how much time you have to invest into research to how interested you are in planning. That being said, if planning your own trip sounds interesting to you – there is no limit to the amount of information available to you online. Moreover, there are many discount travel sites, which can help you secure discounts equal to or greater than those offered by travel agents. Because making this decision is no walk in the park, we are going to explore some of these issues – with hopes of helping you make the right decision for you.

Interest

The first thing you need to take into account when trying to determine whether or not to hire a travel agent is you and your spouse's interest in doing research. Planning a trip requires you to invest hours into researching locations, hotels, activities, sites, plane tickets and much more. Thankfully, the internet now allows anyone to act as their own travel agent. However, if you and your spouse are not interested in investing a significant amount of time into research – than a travel agent might be the right choice.

Time

All of the research, which was mentioned above, can be done by anyone. However, you need to be able to invest several hours to doing the research. If time is something you cannot spare, either because your work is to demanding or your family obligations won't allow for it – then a travel agent might be the right decision. However, if you can spare the time, then planning your own trip can be very rewarding.

Budget

While, on the one hand, travel agents can help you save money on flights and hotels, on the other hand, they also need to be paid. Good travel agents can be expensive. Before you begin utilizing a travel agent, make sure to determine their fees. If their fees are within your budget, then the travel agent might be a good fit. However, if their fees are a bit too much for you, then you may want to reconsider.

Budgeting - Know Your Budget and How to Save

Budgeting and finding savings when planning a honeymoon are probably more relevant today than ever before.

Due to a slow economic recovery and looming uncertainty with regard to financial health – many couples are looking for ways to save money on their honeymoons. Moreover, where once people would go beyond their budget to plan the perfect honeymoon, today planning within your means is paramount. Therefore, before you begin planning your honeymoon there are two things you need to determine – your budget and how to save money.

Determining your honeymoon budget can be stressful. If you are like many newlyweds, you do not yet have much in your savings account – don't worry, there are many affordable options. When you begin creating a budget, there are several things that you need to do. First among them is to determine your current savings / available money. When you begin to look into these areas, take into account funds that may be offered to you by your parents, grandparents and other close relatives. Also, keep an eye open for early wedding gifts. The next thing you should do is to determine when you would like to go on your honeymoon. If you begin planning several months in advance you can increase your budget by saving. For example, if you begin planning six months in advance – you can begin adding a few hundred dollars into a savings account. This will help you increase your budget. The next thing you may look at (which is somewhat less advisable) is how much credit you have available to you. You should not use credit if you cannot reasonably pay it back. However, if you can afford to pay, and your card may be used and paid off in a reasonable amount of time, then a credit card can also help you to increase your budget.

Now that you have determined your budget, you can make your money work harder for you by finding and taking advantage of money saving deals. First, by planning your own honeymoon you can save money that would have otherwise gone to a travel agent. Today, all the information you need to plan your honeymoon is on the internet – this can be an incredibly rewarding experience. Next, use discount travel websites like Orbitz. Discount travel sites can not only save you money, but they can help you plan your honeymoon. You can purchase discounted plane tickets for multiple destinations at once. Furthermore, by using the same site you can find great deals on hotels and car rentals. Next, consider traveling during the off season - usually prices drop considerably. Off season traveling can be a lot of fun as well. Most places are much less crowded – which means restaurants and tour guides will cater to you. Moreover, your hotel will be more focused on your happiness, as you will be one of their primary guests. Finally, consider mapping your own site seeing tours. By purchasing guide books and creating your own tour, you will save lots of money on hiring tour guides. Additionally, by creating your own tour, you will be sure to see all of the things you want to visit and none of the things you don't.

How to Choose the Location

There are so many honeymoon destinations to choose from, so how do you decide which location will be the most meaningful, enjoyable honeymoon for the two of you? This can be a difficult question to answer – and there really is no formula for determining the right answer. This is because, not only are no two people the same, but no two couples are the same.

However, here are a few tips on how to best choose a location that will maximize your honeymoon experience as a couple.

Step One – Existing Ideas

Many people often dream about where they would travel if suddenly they had the ability to just pick-up and go. When determining your honeymoon destination – this can be an effective tool. If you and your spouse have been dreaming of a particular place to honeymoon, then you should begin exploring that idea. However, this is dependent upon the fact that you are both interested in this location. If you are not both interested in this location, or if one of you simply does not want to explore this location – then proceed to step two.

Step Two – Activities

One way to help focus on a location is to consider activities which the two of you enjoy doing as a couple. If you can identify a handful of activities you both are looking forward to doing on your honeymoon, than you can begin to hone in on a location. For example, if you both enjoy wine tasting and the atmosphere of plush wineries – then a wine oriented location may be a good option. From this point you can consider options like Napa Valley in California, or one of the many French wineries. Alternatively, if you both enjoy sailing – than an island destination may be right for you.

Step Three – Climate

Many people don't often consider climate, but this is a good way to select destinations. If you are someone who is averse to heat, they you should avoid hot destinations, like a safari honeymoon. On the other hand, if one of you is averse to cold, then a skiing trip may not be the best idea either. Therefore, by determining your ideal climate, you can narrow down you decision.

Step Four – Price

Another way to help narrow down your options is price. If you are planning your honeymoon on a budget, then you automatically create limitations. Budget honeymoons may keep you closer to home, which can help you in determining nice venues. Alternatively, if you are planning on traveling on a budget, you can look for locations that are known to be slightly more affordable.

Step Five – Recommendations

Finally, many people select honeymoon locations based on recommendation of family and friends. Why? Because, human nature is such that we trust the opinions of the people we are closest to. Before you begin your search, begin speaking to your friends and family. Determine where they went for their honeymoons and ask them about their experiences. Would they recommend the location they went to, or not? If so, what stood out to them? If you like what they have to say about a particular location, then it is worth checking further.

Popular Destinations

Honeymooning is an adventure of a lifetime. So many people have chosen to honeymoon in so many different locations, each with their own flavors and cultures. However, some honeymoon destinations stand out amongst their peers. In this article, we are going to explore some popular honeymoon destinations.

Acapulco, Mexico

Acapulco is one of the most popular honeymoon destinations. In fact, this was the honeymoon destination for John and Jackie Kennedy. Acapulco sits on the shores of the Pacific Ocean and offers warm weather (but not too warm), cool, white sandy beaches, great hotels and luxury service. Resorts in Acapulco also offer various activities for their guests, such as swimming, snorkeling, day sailing trips and hiking. Finally, Acapulco is full of fine dining, great service, good drinks and everything at an affordable price.

Lake Louise, Canada

For honeymooners who prefer snow to sun, Lake Louise is a great option. The famous Fairmont Chateau sits on the edge of this glacier fed lake and offers honeymooners a large variety of winter sports activities – including cross-country skiing, dog sledding, snowshoeing and much more. The hotel offers an abundance of relaxing amenities – including a full spa and restaurants. Honeymooners can hire a sleigh to take them on a moonlit sleigh ride through the wilderness. During warmer months, honeymooners can take advantage of the cool lake, horseback riding, whitewater rafting and much more.

Bali, Indonesia

The Island of Bali is home to a beautiful resort called Amankila – which offers honeymooners the trip of a lifetime. Bali is an enchanted destination for honeymooners. The hotel overlooks the Lombok Strait, which provides heart stopping views and rich culture. This destination is not for everyone, but for couples looking for natural beauty and serious relaxation – Bali may have what you are looking for.

Florence, Italy

Florence is an ideal honeymoon location for true romantics. Florence offers centuries of art and culture, delicious food, Italian culture and incredible museums. Furthermore, Florence offers rich history and many romantic cafes. The beauty of visiting Florence, is that it does not have to be your only stop. Often, honeymooners continue on to explore other parts of Italy – soaking up the Mediterranean sun in the process.

Bora Bora, French Polynesia

Bora Bora is a Pacific island surrounded by a lagoon and barrier reef. This destination is a very popular honeymoon spot, hosting many luxury resorts. Famous for its white sand beaches and clear water, honeymooners can enjoy relaxing days on the beach and create a little excitement with active water sports. Many hotels on the island offer bungalows, which rest on the lagoon and feature amenities like glass floor panels, which allow you to see tropical fish without leaving your room.

Hawaii

Hawaii is a chain of islands, all of which have become very popular for honeymooners. There is no shortage of luxury hotels on the islands – all of which feature numerous amenities, gourmet dining and adult only pools. Hawaii is a popular destination because it offers a variety of activities including water sports, hiking and zip lining. Finally, the islands are full of culture, luaus and relaxing beach fronts.

Honeymoon Accommodations

Choosing honeymoon accommodations that are right for you and your spouse can be a bit overwhelming. There simply are so many choices; one can go crazy considering them all. Therefore, we will try to provide some ideas about determining the right accommodations for your honeymoon. Typically, honeymoon accommodations can be put together as full service "packages" or they can be put together piecemeal by you (often there is a middle option, which we will discuss as well). What does a full service package look like? Usually, full service accommodations take care of everything for you. The hotel you stay in will provide you with room service – if you so desire – but they will also provide you three meals a day, activities, drinks and programs. Many full service resorts will help you plan interesting excursions and they will book them for you. Literally everything you need will be a handled by your resort.

The piecemeal option is much more affordable and a lot more rewarding. The general piecemeal option is for you as the couple to book your hotel and all of your activities. That is, the hotel will be happy to give you advice and suggestions, but you will be responsible for booking reservations, etc. Moreover, though your hotel may provide you a complimentary breakfast – most, if not all, meals will be your responsibility. The rewarding and fun aspect of this type of accommodation is that you get to do more of your own exploring. You are able to see things beyond what the hotel may recommend for you. You will have a chance to interact more with the local culture, and try more local restaurants, which your hotel may not recommend for you.

There is also a middle ground. There are honeymoon resorts, which will provide you with all of the amenities you would like, but they are not necessarily included in your stay. This option is nice because it gives you the convenience of choosing to take advantage of your hotel amenities, without feeling like you cannot do your own exploring. The ideal scenario, with this type of resort, is that you will spend part of your time enjoying your hotel amenities and part of your trip will be spent exploring local restaurants and activities.

The question now is, how do you decide which option is for you. There are several factors, which need to be considered. First of which is the budget. Full service resorts are pricy. If you are not in a position to afford "full service" then you should consider one of the other two options.

Next, you should consider preference. How much do you and your spouse enjoy planning your trips? How involved do you like to be in selecting your activities? If the answer is very, then you can save a lot of money by creating your own trip – i.e. using the piecemeal option. If the answer is somewhat, than you would be doing yourselves a huge service by choosing the middle option – this way the onus is not entirely on you. Finally, if you want to be completely pampered – then you will maximize your experience with full service accommodations.

Activities

Your honeymoon has finally arrived! After all of the wedding planning, all of the planning and anticipation for the honeymoon – here it is! Now that you have arrived to your ideal honeymoon destination, what are you guys going to do? Thankfully, there are many activities that you can choose from – if you so choose, there will never be a dull moment. In this article, we are going to explore different activities, which may be just what you're looking for. Of course, honeymoon activities are very much dependent upon your honeymoon destination. Therefore this will be a snap shot of different activities, which may not be available to everyone.

Snorkeling

Snorkeling is a very popular beach / ocean activity. Snorkeling basically allows you to swim with your face submerged for long periods of time – without all of the heavy gear needed for scuba diving. Snorkeling can be a very romantic activity, which couples can share together. By swimming in shallow waters, couples can share the beauty and splendor of tropical reef environments. This is a fun activity, which will create lasting memories.

Day Cruise

Another popular beach / ocean activity is day cruising. Usually, day cruises are between 5 and 8 hours long, and take place on a medium size catamaran – a multi-hulled sail boat. These trips usually include good music, swimming and towards the end of the trip – an open bar. Day cruises are incredibly relaxing and a lot of fun.

Skiing

A popular honeymoon activity in snowy destinations is skilling, which is a fun, adventurous activity that couples can share together. If you are both expert skiers, then enjoy the slopes. If you are just learning how to ski, then this can be a great learning and bonding experience. Most of all, the magic of snowcapped mountains can take anyone's breath away. Who else would you rather share this with, then your new husband or wife?

Hot Air Ballooning

Believe it or not, riding in a hot air balloon is a more common honeymoon activity than you may think. Floating several hundred feet above the ground creates one of the most beautiful, romantic views you will ever see. Moreover, a nice hot air balloon has enough space for you to bring a nice picnic basket. You can enjoy delicious cheeses and tasty wines, while viewing the world from the sky.

Room Service

True, room service may not be an "activity," but this is your honeymoon after all. You can't spend all of your time outside! Make sure that you don't forget to enjoy your time together. Sleep late, order room service and spend as much time in each other's arms as possible. Vacations like this don't come around every day, so take advantage of it while you can.

Hiking

If you and your spouse are outdoorsy, then hiking is a great activity. Taking a long hike through the gorgeous wilderness is an experience you won't soon forget. A great way to make the hike more romantic is to bring a bottle of wine and some snacks along. When you find a nice view, or a private spot along the way, take a break. Have some wine and soak in the nature.

Making Reservations

Making reservations sounds like a no brainer – but they can be the thing that saves your honeymoon (not that your honeymoon needs saving). Why are reservations so important? There really are several reasons. There are many levels or stages to your honeymoon planning. First, you must decide on a location. Once you have a location, you must book a plane ticket – buying a plane ticket is akin to a reservation. That is, don't wait until the last minute. True, buying plane tickets the week before you fly can be a great money saver – but don't take this approach with your honeymoon. Why? There is no guarantee that you will get on a flight. Furthermore, if you wait until the last minute, this can create a lot of stress. Therefore, to avoid stress and potentially not get a flight – buy your tickets early.

The next step is reserving a hotel room. Make sure that you do your research early and that you reserve your room early. The closer you get to your trip, the harder and more expensive it will be to get a room. Again, pre-honeymoon stress can be a big factor. You want to be certain that you have a place to stay when you land – if you wait until the last minute, this lack of a guarantee can be very stressful. So book your room early. Finally, make sure to follow up with the hotel in order to ensure that they have your reservation on file.

Now that you have booked your flight and reserved your hotel room, this brings us to your actual trip. Being spontaneous is a lot of fun. However, being too spontaneous too frequently can lead to arguments – you don't want this on your honeymoon. Therefore, leave yourselves some room to be spontaneous, but be sure to make reservations for the big activities of your day. That is, if you plan on going on a tour during the day, make a reservation in advance. By making reservations for your main activities, you are better able to plan your time. Moreover, early reservations for activities can often get you discounted prices – make sure to look into this. That being said, make sure not to overbook yourselves.

When it comes to eating out, reservations can be a life saver. If there is a nice restaurant you would like to go to, don't put yourselves through the disappointment of being turned away. Make a reservation. That being said, eating out can be a great way to incorporate spontaneity into your honeymoon. It can be a lot of fun spending time exploring your honeymoon destination and choosing a place to sit down for dinner at random. However, try to avoid this on an empty stomach, because if you don't find something suitable, you may lose patience.

Finally, try to understand that making reservations are important. But they do not, necessarily, lock you into your activity. If you feel like you want to avoid reservations because too much advanced planning may eat into your vacation freedom, try not to think like that – you can always cancel your reservation.

Making Memories

Your honeymoon will be a vacation of a lifetime – so make sure to live every moment to its fullest. If you ensure that you have the best time you possibly can, you can rest assured that you will have memories that will last you a lifetime. But, just in case one or two moments slip by, here are a few suggestions on how to make some wonderful honeymoon memories.

First, don't be embarrassed to be a little silly. Relax and have a good time. Anytime you are able to joke with your loved one, you create an impression. There is nothing stronger than laughter- so make each other laugh.

Next, try to do something out of the ordinary. Be adventurous. When life becomes routine, we don't remember the details of our days. However, when something unusual happens – that sticks with us. Therefore, try to do something that you would not usually do, something uncharacteristic. This will leave a lasting impression for both you and your spouse. For example, if you are afraid of heights, challenge yourselves to go ziplining – this will be something you never forget.

Another way to create memories is to create intimacy. When a couple is intimate with each other, the body releases chemicals which heighten our senses towards our spouse. This also helps us remember. The more intimate a couple is, the closer they feel with one another. This closeness creates a lasting impression, which is imprinted on our minds. What kind of intimacy is needed to create this kind of memory? The truth is, not much. The smallest things, which are affectionate and meaningful, have huge impacts on our psyche. Something as little as holding hands can transform a normal walk into a magical stroll. Therefore, be intimate, hold hands and kiss a lot.

Next, create as many romantic experiences as you can. Romance is a great way to create lasting memories. Romance does not have to be complicated, something as simple as a candle lit dinner can burn a beautiful image into your minds.

Take advantage of your hotel and the restaurants they offer, call ahead and reserve a romantic table. Take walks under the moonlight, and retire to your room for champagne and quality alone time.

Another way to create memories is to make little surprises for one another. We, as humans, love to get little surprises from the ones we love. A small surprise can be a little gift, or simply bringing your spouse a cup of coffee in the morning. Make sure to be thoughtful - the more thought you put into something, the more meaning it has. And the more meaning it has, the more ingrained it will be in your memory.

Finally, a great way to create memories is to have a record of the things you do. As they say, "a picture is worth a thousand words." Make sure to take a lot of pictures. Take pictures of one another, take selfies and most of all do not be embarrassed to ask a stranger to take a picture of the two of you together. Though it might be a little uncomfortable to ask, twenty years from now you will be glad that you did.

To Do List

Creating a to-do list sounds like a daunting, boring task. But, this "task" can save you a lot of hassle. It is very much worth your while to create detailed to do lists for the various stages of your honeymoon. Why? Primarily because you don't want to forget something important. Imagine that you arrive in Hawaii and you forgot your swim suit truc, this is an easy fix, but it is still a hassle. Moreover, imagine forgetting to do something important like paying your credit card bill before you left on your trip. These types of events can create a lot of stress and unnecessary aggravation, which could put a damper on your trip. Therefor make sure to create a good to do list for every stage of your trip.

First, you need to create a to-do list for the things that need to be done before you leave on your honeymoon. Think very carefully about all of the tasks you need to "have in-order" before you leave. For example, make sure to include in your list paying all of your bills or setting up an automatic payment. Make sure to include requesting time off from work, etc. Additionally, make sure that you include other things that may be relevant. For example, if you are taking your honeymoon several months after your wedding – make sure to include finishing your thank you cards before you leave.

The next stage is to create a packing list for you and your spouse. Make sure that you take the time to seriously consider what it is you will need to bring with you. This list will very much be dictated by where you are going. For example, if you are going to a cold destination, you need to bring warm clothes and vice versa. Additionally, you should try to determine how many evenings will require you to wear dressier clothing. You don't want to over pack, but you also don't want to be underdressed. Next, taking into account how many activities will require you to have more rugged or athletic gear. If you are spending everyday poolside, no problem. But if you are planning on hiking – you may need to pack for that. Next, include in your packing list electronic devices that you many need (note that if you are going to a foreign country, you may need to purchase an adaptor).

Finally, create a to-do list / itinerary for your trip. By having a general plan, you will feel more organized and will know how to prepare for each day. Your itinerary does not have to detail every minute of the day, however it should include a general overview of what you are doing that day. For example, if the first day of your trip you will be hiking in the morning, having lunch, then relaxing by the beach until dinner. Then make sure to give approximate times and note if you have any reservations. The most important part of a to-do list is to keep you organized. If you plan too much, then you will feel trapped. But, if you plan too little, you may miss out on great adventures. So do yourselves a favor and make a to-do list.

SAYING THANK YOU

Saying Thank You
after Your Wedding

Congratulations! You are now the happiest newlyweds on the block. Thanks to your family and friends, you and your new husband or wife have just had the most magical night of your lives. You stayed up until 2am dancing, laughing and fondly staring into the eyes of your one true love.

Now, however, the time has come to get back to reality – to come back to earth from cloud nine; and, of course, the first thing you should think about is preparing your thank you cards. Why should this be such a high priority? The simple answer is etiquette, yes, etiquette – that word your grandmother and mother have been throwing around for the better part of your life. However, beyond etiquette – or said slightly differently – the reason for this practice and why it is good etiquette, is simply because you love your family and friends and should want to thank them from the bottom of your heart. The simple reason for any thank you is to express your gratitude for something kind someone else has done for you. In the case of a wedding, to remind your friends and family that you truly do appreciate all the help, advice and friendship they have given you over the years – and of course to thank them for the lovely gifts.

Now that we have discussed the importance of thank you notes, we can delve a little deeper into thank you etiquette. First of all, let's go back in time to before the wedding. During this time you probably had a few parties, where you received some pretty lovely gifts. That is right; gifts that you received at engagement parties, bridal showers and any other shower require thank you cards. Moreover, the early wedding gifts you received also require thank you cards. The question is when to send them.

As a general rule, thank you cards for gifts received from engagement parties and showers should be sent within two or three weeks of the event. Additionally, early wedding gifts should be sent before your wedding date. There are two primary reasons for this custom. The first is courtesy. Your friends and family have put a lot of thought and effort into the gifts that they got you. They want to know that you appreciated the time end effort they put in − they also want to know that you appreciated the gift itself. The second reason is simple planning. As you already know, the months before your wedding are incredibly busy. The more things you push off, the busier (and the more stressed) you are going to become. By forcing yourself to finish the thank you notes early, you will be alleviating the potential stress and backlog of thank you cards that are to come.

Finally, with regard to thank you card etiquette as it relates to the wedding gifts you received on the day or your wedding, standard practice is to have these thank you cards mailed within two to three months. This is because, on the one hand everyone knows it takes a long time to write several hundred thank you cards. But at the same time anything beyond three months creates an impression that you just don't care. It is a good idea to order your thank you cards while you're making all your other arrangements for your wedding.

Thank You Cards

Though you may have thought the wedding whirlwind would die down at the end of your wedding, or at least after your honeymoon, the truth is it hasn't quite stopped yet. The moment you got back from you honeymoon you might have been expecting to settle into normal married life and to begin playing with the mountain of wedding gifts sitting in your guest room. However, your friends and family – who went out of their way to ensure you would have a mountain of gifts in your guest room – need acknowledgment. Therefore, you need to hold out for just a bit longer, in order to write a couple hundred thank you cards. Don't worry, though it seems daunting, we will help you with some time saving thank you card writing tips.

Preparation

Believe it or not, you begin preparing for your thank you card-writing marathon when you start ordering and sending invitations. Normally, when you order invitations you will receive thank you cards and envelopes – this is what you will be sending out. Additionally, by the time you are ordering your invitations, you probably have a hard list of guests and their addresses. Make sure to keep this list - you will need it again. If you are having names and addressing printed on your wedding invitation envelopes, have them printed on the thank you card envelopes as well – this will save you a lot of time.

Next, make sure to keep a list of all of the people you invited to your wedding. Leave a space on this list to write down what each person gave you as a gift. This will help you streamline the thank you card writing process and it will ensure that you are thanking the right person for the right gift.

Writing Your Thank you Cards

First, keep in mind that no one can write two hundred thank you cards in one sitting. That is okay. Try to pace yourself. Moreover, if you have the opportunity, write your thank you cards as the gifts come in. Next, keep a list of envelopes and thank you cards nearby. Also, be sure to keep the list of names, addresses and gifts nearby – organization will save you a lot of time. Next, begin drafting your notes. Try to be as specific as possible in your note, this tells the recipient that you care enough to acknowledge the gift. If you receive money, you do not necessarily need to specify the exact amount – you can use language such as, "the generous check", instead.

Be sure to keep a thank you card deadline – the date by which all of your thank you cards must be mailed. This will help you stay focused. Be sure that you write all of your thank you cards with either black or blue ink – and never use stationary with your maiden name only (it is customary to use stationary with both of your names and that same family name). Finally, be sure to write thank you cards to guests who attended the wedding but did not bring gifts. It can be difficult for people to attend weddings and this effort deserves acknowledgment.

WEDDING PLANNING APPS

Apps That Make Your Wedding Planning Easier

As the modern bride becomes more attached to her smartphone, wedding planning tools become more convenient. Today there are many different wedding planning smartphone apps, which can be used to help streamline your wedding planning process. With new and changing technology, brides can do away with old wedding planning procedures and get access to an almost unlimited amount of information from their phones (this information can be filtered and limited in order to provide you with only relevant information). We will take a look at some of these apps and what they have to offer:

Our Wedding Planner

Our Wedding Planner is an app that allows multiple people to take part in the planning process. The app features a budget guide, which will automatically calculate how much you can afford to spend on each area of your wedding based on your total budget. The app allows you to manage you guest list, budget and vendors all on your smartphone. This particular app has a high customer rating – with many customers praising it's budgeting gadget.

Appy Couple

Appy Couple focuses on connecting the engaged couple with their friends and family. The app is designed to ensure that your wedding guests have everything they need at their fingertips. This includes a social network, access to the couple's wedding website and more. This app has mixed reviews

Brides Wedding Planner

Brides Wedding Planner can provide you with hundreds of honeymoon destination ideas, dress designs, and venue options. The app provides you with hundreds of images, which are meant to inspire you and help you come up with design ideas. This information can be shared with your friends and family. Additionally, the app has a wedding countdown – which counts down the number of days until you will be saying "I Do".

Wedding Happy

Wedding Happy offers a lot of functionality. The app begins by determining how much time you have to plan your wedding - in turn giving you suggested deadlines for important milestones. Additionally, the app has a wedding countdown and an interactive calendar. Finally, the app has a vendor management gadget, which allows you to manage vendor contact information and more. This has very positive reviews.

Wedding Countdown

Wedding Countdown is another such app that offers users many different functions. The highlight of the app include its flexible countdown units, which work in any combination of years, months, weeks, days, hours, minutes and seconds, and even special units like "heartbeats" and "kisses" - "3 months 15 days" or "82 kisses". The app filters photos for you so you can see pictures of you and your love. You can personalize your wedding countdown with your favorite song. The app also provides post wedding functionality. For example it allows you to track your anniversary and re-live your wedding day. Finally this app offers a lot of extra features, including slides shows and multiple countdowns, i.e. countdowns to bridal showers and engagement parties.

The Knot Wedding Planner

The Knot is meant to be a personal wedding planner. The idea for the app is to help you become inspired for your wedding by planning the details, and booking everything in one place! If you have an account with The Knot, the app will automatically sync with your tools on your account. The app also features over 50,000 ideas from past weddings, which can be filtered by category and colors. You can find vendors and speak with them through the apps inbox − the app offers a list of over 250,000 wedding vendors. Moreover, the app will help you stay on task by utilizing the wedding checklist. You can personalize your app and create a budget as needed − the app features a budget tool. Finally, you can save store information, pictures and much more. This app has average reviews.

Pro Wedding Planner

Pro Wedding Planner claims to be the most advanced wedding planner available − and perhaps it is. The app allows you to create seating charts in minutes by importing you own table map, adding guests to tables all with a simple drag and drop tool. Additionally, the app will allow you to view that seating arrangements in augmented reality. The app allows you to manage all of you guests from one source. You can control and monitor your RSVPs, invitations, thank you cards and gifts. This information can be easily imported to Google Docs or MS Excel. Next, the app allows you to track your progress and budget. This is done by assigning tasks and being able to quickly see how they are progressing. The budgeting tool allows you to keep track of your budget and make adjustments where necessary. This app comes highly recommended.

Wedding Flowers Mood board

The Wedding Flowers Mood board app helps you design the image you want for your wedding bouquet. The app helps you through a large selection of images and tips, which help you decide the shape of your bouquet, the style, the color, and also look. This is based on the season your wedding is going to take place – as not all flowers are available all of the time. You are able to select the photos you like and add them to your "moodboard" and you can include notes on each one. You have the ability to take your own photos and add them to your " moodboard" as well. You can share you moodboard with your friends, your florist or your wedding planner. This app has a high customer satisfaction rate.

Wedding Party

Wedding Party is an Android app that allows you to collect photos from all of your guests and "help them stay connected and in the loop as you count down to your big day". The app will automatically organize your photos by event, keeping track of every moment from your engagement to your honeymoon – these photos will go into beautiful albums. This app is primarily focused on pictures and videos – and has a solid customer satisfaction rating.

Wedding Wire

The Wedding Wire planning app can easily and seamlessly link your wedding checklist, budget, guest list, and the rest of the tools you are utilizing on the Wedding Wire website with the site itself. This app gives you access to over 200,000 local wedding vendors and over 2 million wedding vendor reviews. If you are looking for ideas, this app allows you to browse thousands of wedding photos in order to get the wedding ideas you need. Moreover, this app has a built in community of engaged couples, where you can get advice from other couples and newlyweds. This advice can help to steer you in the right directions. Some of the tools the app features are its planning tool, vender tool and its photo gallery tool. This app has high reviews.

Zola Registry

The Zola Registry app is an app designed to help you create your ultimate wedding registry. The Zola app allows you to register for the leading brands to memory-making experiences, honeymoon funds, and more. The app allows you to create and manage your Zola wedding registry from virtually anywhere. Additionally, the app will notify you when someone has purchase an item from your registry. The app allows you to create your entire registry from your phone – you don't have to go to a store. You can personalize your registry with picture or reasons / ideas for having or using a particular item. You can add gift as often as you want and you can browse entire selections of gifts from different stores. Finally, if you are at a store, you can use you cell phone camera to scan a bar code and add that item to your registry. This app has high reviews.

Pinterest

Pinterest is an app that helps you plan events. The app allows you to pin things that you like, such as wedding ideas. The app will then make similar recommendations to you. This can help you come up with creative ideas you had not yet thought of. Because the app works on an algorithm – typically the things that it shows you are things similarly to what you have already been searching. That being said, there have been many negative reviews about this app. Many people feel that the app is only giving suggestions, which were sponsored by other vendors. This may be true – but if you are looking for new and exciting ideas, this can still be a great tool for you. Just keep in mind to be open about your expectations and what you are looking for.

Evernote

Evernote is an app that will sync to all of your devices. This app is great for making to-do lists, especially when multiple people are involved. Each person can have access to the same list and check off their progress – allowing everyone else to see what they have accomplished. This can be a great wedding planning tool, as it allows all individuals involved in the wedding planning process be on the same page.

ADDITIONAL THINGS TO KEEP IN MIND

Stress! Stress! Stress!

Before a wedding can happen, there almost always must first be a long period of stress and tension. There is so much to organize, as we have already seen. While there may well be plenty of excitement and happiness, the opposite emotions are quite natural in these situations, as well. There are times when it can feel very difficult to go on planning your wedding. All of the stress and hassle can get on top of you very easily. You will find that in every single relationship, there is at least a small amount of conflict that will take place between the two partners before they get married. There is no way to avoid it; what matters is how you deal with it.

The main problem is emotional investment. You are both looking forward to getting married, and you both want it to happen. You love each other very much. For this reason, you are going to invest a lot of emotion into every decision. This is especially the case if at least one of you wants everything to be just right. You will get emotional over things that seem silly, like the flowers being just slightly the wrong shade of pink. To anyone else, and for any other occasion, it would seem as though you were reacting in a way that was over the top and unrealistic. But this is a wedding, and more than that, it is your wedding. The behavior that would otherwise seem irrational is therefore explained by the importance of the event in your life.

You can also consider that things will certainly become heated if one of you is more involved in the wedding planning than the other. Because this is the bulk of the stressful work, the person who takes the most of it on is going to be the one feeling the most under pressure. They may become upset if they feel like their partner is not pulling their weight. On the other hand, their partner may also become upset if they feel like they are not being allowed enough say in the wedding and the big decisions around it. It is important to find a balance that suits both of you.

When it comes to situations like these, sometimes the only way forward is to take it one small step at a time. You probably feel as though big tasks are completely beyond you, and that you can only do something very small every day. But even by making progress in this way, you can get there. Just pick out one thing that needs to be done each day – you can even write yourself a schedule for the weeks and months ahead if this helps to keep you on track. Then you can simply go through and cross off each one as it comes. By taking one step at a time you can make real progress. Perhaps all that you can do is to make one phone call or decide on one thing. But that is one more thing crossed off your list, and the rest of the list will not grow. When the wedding is approaching nearer, you will still be making progress, so you can get everything sorted out before it is too late.

However, even doing that is not really enough to make sure that you will not end up fighting over something. At the end of the day, it is bound to happen. There is no avoiding it. You must simply take a deep breath after you have had an argument. If one of you ends up crying, then the other should make sure to comfort them, instead of letting things go any further. You must be sensitive to the fact that this is a busy and stressful time for both of you. When the argument is over, just take some time to reassess. Remember that if you did not love each other, you would not be getting married. Also remember that after this, there will be many happy years ahead of you, with the wonderful memories of your wedding to make them all the sweeter. Everyone gets upset and argues before their wedding. It's just natural!

The Bridezilla Mindset

We have all heard the term "bridezilla". This is used in a tongue in cheek manner, and occasionally in a way that is actually quite hurtful. No one would like to think of herself as being a bridezilla, but at some point or other, it is quite likely that someone will use it around you. Even if they are only joking, this can be something that makes you quite upset. It may be necessary to mentally prepare yourself for this happening, so that it does not feel quite as hurtful if and when you do hear it.

The idea behind bridezilla is of a bride who has gone crazy from the stress of the wedding planning. She must have everything her way, and will go on a rampage if something does not go to plan. She argues with her mother in law, and has no problem with yelling at anyone. The worst instance of a bridezilla manifesting can be seen at wedding dress sales, where women can physically fight over who gets the best dresses.

All of this is a stereotype, and it may in many cases be exaggerated. But if you do happen to exhibit some of this behavior, it may well be that no one could blame you. After all, when we live in a culture where a woman can be described as a bridezilla just for wanting something to go well, it seems like we are actually encouraging this kind of over the top behavior. We see it in films and TV shows, and it is widely discussed in cultural settings. Therefore, is it any surprise if some people turn out to act this way?

In many cases, what really happens is that friends and family are not supportive or understanding enough of your needs and emotions. This leads to them calling you a bridezilla over small things and not allowing you to have the time to vent that you need. Eventually, all of these accusations and the lack of support will end up driving you crazy. It is a vicious cycle and can certainly make you feel unloved, unsupported, and like you want to act the way that you say you are. It can be a very uncomfortable and stressful time for you, so you will want to make sure that you get the support and help that you need.

If you feel that you are in danger of becoming a real bridezilla, it may be time to sit down with your partner or anyone else who has been a problem. Explain to them that you feel as though you need more from them (or less, as the case may be). Tell them how stressed you are and how much this wedding means to you. With any luck, they will be more supportive in future and will be more understanding of any reactions that you may have. This will help you to calm down more quickly.

Cold Feet Syndrome

Another saying that gets tossed around a lot is "cold feet." It might be used as a joke, to suggest that you are thinking about cancelling the wedding if you do something that might lead in this direction. It might be said as a statement of fact, such as the saying that all men get cold feet on the day of the wedding.

Actually, it is a strange phenomenon, and it is not as cut and dried as everybody seems to think. First of all, not everyone happens to get cold feet. If they do, it does not always happen on the day of the wedding – it can be months before. You should also know that getting cold feet is perfectly natural, but that you should carefully consider these feelings. Do this just in case something lies inside them that has a basis in truth.

"Cold feet" is the idea of wanting to cancel the wedding or run away from the altar because you now feel that the marriage would be a bad idea. Some people might also describe it as having second thoughts. This is natural because marriage, while a happy and wonderful experience, can also be quite intimidating. Committing to one person for the rest of your life is a really big deal. If you did not stop and think about it seriously, considering the negatives as well as the positives, then you might not be taking it seriously enough.

However, this does not mean that you should always listen to yourself when you are feeling down in the dumps and doubting everything. This can simply come out of the stress and unhappiness caused by wedding planning. When you have a fight with your significant other over the color of the tablecloths, you can be left feeling like it isn't meant to be. However, this is when you must put things aside for a minute and think about it. Is it really worth calling off the wedding and throwing away your relationship just because you do not like the same type of tablecloth?

One of the best ways to deal with cold feet is to try and imagine your life without your significant other. Rather than fantasizing about the best possible things, look at it in a realistic way if you can. Think about what you would do with your day, how you would spend your time, and whom you would talk to. Chances are, you cannot really imagine life without them. You love them so much that it would be a pointless or joyless existence. That is how you know that you are not making a mistake, and that getting married is the right thing to do.

Besides, if you want to calm yourself down a little, think of it this way. Marriage is not something that has to be forever. In an ideal world, of course it will. But if you make a mistake, you can change things later on. Nothing is final.

Your Wedding is Not a Hassle or Imposition

Remember that your big day is very important not only to you, but also to your family and your close friends. It is a big life event, and they should be able to respect and admire this. More than that, they should want to be a part of it. This means that your wedding should not be an imposition, either on the day itself or during the planning phase beforehand. Do not feel awkward or as though you have to suit everyone else – it is YOUR day, and that is what counts.

No one should make you feel as though you are imposing on him or her when they come to your wedding. To be invited is an honor, something that you do not extend to absolutely everyone. It is down to them whether they come or not. Do not let them make you feel as though you are messing up their day by having such an inconvenient event planned. This is all about you and celebrating your move into a life together. If there is someone who wants to make it a big problem, then perhaps they ought not to be invited at all. This goes for anyone who complains about the location, day, time, and so on. It is their choice to attend or not!

Remember also that you are not obliged to plan your wedding around anyone else and their needs. If you have someone, cannot make the date because they are going to another party, then so what? They will have to decide which event they wish to go to the most. The only people that your wedding must suit are yourselves. You should consider your parents and close family members, and those who are to be part of the wedding party. Everyone else is an invited guest, not someone for whom the whole event should be rearranged.

This also goes for any help that you need. For example, you might ask one of your siblings to help out by being an usher, a bridesmaid, or one of the groomsmen. This is something that they should be honored to be asked to do. If they are grumpy about it and do not want to put the effort in, then you should consider taking them out of the wedding party. It is up to them to refuse, and you can always find someone else. If anyone makes you feel as though you are putting them out, then there are two ways for you to go. If you do not mind confrontation, then you can point out to them that this is perhaps the most important day of your life, and that you are not asking much. Alternatively, you can just find someone else to help.

Really, this is a time when you may begin to find out who your real friends and supportive family members are. If they cannot be bothered to help out with your wedding, then they are not worth bothering with.

Expect the Unexpected

One of the biggest things that you might worry about when the big day finally comes around is actually getting through it. There is still so much to organize at the last minute, and there are so many things that can go wrong. You do not want to face any negative possibilities, but it is absolutely possible that everything will fall apart. So how do you get through the day – without losing your mind?

The first step is to remember that no matter what happens, this is your wedding day. It is special and it will be memorable, no matter what. Even if something does not go entirely as planned, you will still be married by the end of the day, and you will still cherish your fantastic memories. Should something go wrong on the day, it may feel like the end of the world. But in twenty years' time, you will be laughing when you tell the story of how exactly the groom managed to turn up to the ceremony with a black eye.

The only way to keep control of yourself and survive the day without going crazy is to let go a little. Up until now, everything has been about planning and making it perfect. You have done as much as you can to ensure that that will be the case. Now is the time to just enjoy it and let it all happen. You have your wedding party to help if things do go wrong.

While we are on the subject, there is nothing wrong with asking everyone to pitch in just a little more on the day. You may have already enlisted them to help you out, but that might not be enough. If you are looking for a chance to relax and actually enjoy your wedding day, you might have to ask someone to help out in a few areas.

You may ask one of your bridesmaids, for example, to track down the wedding cars and make sure that everyone is ready to go on time. This will allow you simply to get yourself ready and make sure that your hair and makeup are done. You may ask one of the groomsmen to help out with getting people to the right seats at the reception. It could well be that you can have him standing beside the seating chart and just making sure that everyone finds the right place.

Whatever you need help with, do not be afraid to ask. After all, it is your wedding day! If you cannot ask for someone to do you a favor now, then when can you? Make sure that you are grateful after the wedding: it is customary to give small gifts to the wedding party, and you may decide to give them something a little extra if they do pull their weight on the day when it matters the most.

Have Some People in Charge

The secret to maintaining control on your wedding day is to have a solid plan in place beforehand. Everyone should know where they need to be, what they need to be doing, and who will be helping them at all times of the day. This will give you the best chance of making sure that everything runs to plan, and stays on schedule as well.

On the day itself, you should appoint a few key people who are in charge of other areas. The maid of honor could be in charge of the bridesmaids and making sure that they are doing what they are supposed to, for example. The best man can do the same for the groomsmen. Someone else can be in charge of the ushers and any children who are involved with the ceremony, and so on. So long as you have someone in charge of every area, you do not have to get in there and micromanage by yourself. You can trust them to look after everything else on your behalf.

These heads can also report back to you if something goes wrong or a quick decision needs to be made. Alternatively, they can try to fix the problem themselves so that you do not have to endure the stress. It is up to you how you handle things. Just remember that you do not need to have a finger on every pulse in order to maintain control. Your wedding party can do that for you.

Imperfection is Expected

Sooner or later, something will end up going wrong. It could be incredibly trivial, like a rose petal falling off before you get to the ceremony, or one of the entrees not being cooked through at the reception. It could be something major, such as a rip in the dress or your hair being ruined by the rain. In each case, however, the thing to do is not to panic or to declare that the whole day has been ruined. Instead, it is time to take a deep breath, smile anyway, and enjoy your wedding day.

Imperfection is fine. In fact, it is to be expected. There is no reason why you should end up feeling as though it has all gone down the drain if one thing is not perfect. These little imperfections could turn out to be the things that make the day all the more special. Instead of stressing out about them, embrace them. Realize that they may well be just the thing that you needed.

Perhaps the badly cooked entree makes the rest of the meal taste so much better, or the rose petal was one that looked out of place anyway. Maybe you can bond with your mother while the dress is repaired, or style it up to create a new and more exciting look. Maybe the wet look reminds your new husband of a time when you got caught in the rain together, and makes everything all the more perfect for him. Imperfection can be perfectly fine.

Enjoy Your Wedding Day

After planning the wedding has taken over your life for so long, it can be easy to get lost in the details. You can obsess over every little thing, trying to make sure that everything is perfect. You start to micromanage. You no longer trust other people to take care of the things that they have been assigned to. You feel that you need to oversee everything so that there cannot be any mistakes. Does all of this sound familiar? If so, you may need to learn how to take a step back.

It is very easy to stay wrapped up in those details all the way through the wedding. Instead of enjoying the journey to the ceremony, you stress about your clothes or the fact that you are running a few minutes late. When you enter the ceremony you worry about whether the flowers have been sorted out properly. Getting to the reception only opens you up to endless worries about food and drink, entertainment, and seating arrangements.

But while you are thinking about all of this, you are missing the most special day of your life.

When it comes to the day itself, you need to let go of any worries and let other people handle them. It is time to stop thinking about the months that you have spent in preparation and the things that could have gone wrong. It is time to stop thinking about what might go wrong in the next minutes and hours. You just have to be there and enjoy everything as it happens.

It is very likely that things will, in fact, go wrong. That is perfectly normal. In fact, it would not be real life without a few hiccups. But the point is that you want to make sure that you enjoy it anyway. Perhaps you will trip as you leave your ceremony, and your stumble will be caught in the wedding pictures. So what? No one gets hurt, you have a funny picture to look at later on, and you can carry on just the same. Almost any hiccup in your wedding can be treated the same way. If there is a mistake in the seating plans, then it will get worked out. Should the food not be perfect, the taste is only momentary, and you will not remember it forever. There is really nothing to worry about once it has all been set up and put into motion.

If you find yourself being rushed along with the day instead of really experiencing it, then take a moment to stop. Take a deep breath, and look around you. See everything. Think about how you are feeling. Look at your new spouse and realize that this is it – this is your wedding day. Now is the time to be happy and to live in the moment. Capture all of these fantastic memories. You can examine everything in full later!

After the Wedding

Once the dust has settled, everything will look a little different. The champagne bottles will be empty. The confetti will be sticking to the floor. Everyone will have sore feet from dancing and sore heads from staying up all night to celebrate. You will eventually retire to your bridal suite, spending the first night together after the ceremony.

And you will be married.

Here's the first thing that we have to talk about after the wedding. Even though the wedding night is something that always gets built up as something really special, it is not the case for everyone. Sometimes, you will just be ready to go to sleep and nothing else. Think about it: the last few months have been hectic, all culminating in this one massive day. You are exhausted. Your body aches. The wedding dress is heavy, the shoes hurt your feet, and just like everyone else, you've had too much champagne. You are full of buffet food and wedding cake. Is it any wonder if you just want to get some rest?

If the wedding night does not quite go according to plan, then do not worry. You will still have the next night, and the night after that, and the night after that. You are married! You get to spend the rest of your lives together. A delay of one night does not mean a thing. Plus, soon you will be off on honeymoon. That is when you will really start to have some fun.

For most couples, going on honeymoon right after the wedding is exactly the tonic that they need. They do not have to worry about the ceremony and more and all of the planning that went with it. There is time to sign off for a while, to stay away from phones and the internet, and just relax. It is also time to explore this newfound passion for one another. Even though all that has happened is the signing of a piece of paper, everything will feel new and exciting. You will be just getting used to the idea of being husband and wife, and when you hear someone describe you as Mr. and Mrs., you will most likely be giddy.

You should really try to enjoy your time on honeymoon. This is a well-deserved break, something that makes up for all of the time and stress that you spent on the wedding. It is time to spend just with each other. There are no family members or friends around now. It is just the two of you. Make sure to enjoy it while it lasts!

When you return home, there are a few more things to take care of. The first thing is to make sure that your names are changed, if necessary. There are a lot of areas in which your name is used, and which must be updated in order to keep things running smoothly. If the bride is taking her husband's name, then this will need to be reflected in any official documentation. She will need a new passport, and may need an update to her driving license and other official licenses as well. The name on her bank account and associated with any legal documents must be changed. At work, her payroll entry and even her email signature must be updated. There is a lot to sort out in this area alone.

Any vendors who have not yet been paid should be paid in full at this time, too. They are professionals who make their living from these events, and so you should pay them promptly, even though you do have a lot to think about. It is then time to keep an eye on and chase up anyone who owes you anything as well. Chief among these will be the photographer. They will need to work on your images and get the proofs out to you so that you can see what to expect in your wedding album. This will also give you a chance to decide whether you would like to have any prints made.

Your photographer should hopefully have already given you an estimate of when they will be able to get the images out to you. If not, chase them down now and ask them for a guideline time period. You will then know when it is time to chase them up again if they still have not delivered. The same goes for anyone in your wedding party who was also taking photos. Make it clear that you want to see them all as soon as possible so that you can get them up on social media, save them to your own albums, and enjoy looking at them.

One loose end that you may wish to tie up is the wedding dress. It is time to decide what to do with it! Some people have different approaches. For example, it has been traditional to keep hold of a wedding dress. You would store it away with mothballs in order to keep it safe. Then in the future, you might hand it down to future generations, whether for them to wear or simply as a keepsake. Nowadays, you also have the option of doing a trash the dress shoot. This is when you get a photographer out to take pictures of you that will almost certainly ruin the dress. You could walk through mud, go into a lake or river, set it on fire, spray it with paints, or whatever you wanted. This is supposed to be a fun and enjoyable way to use something that has outlived its purpose. It is also a statement of intent – that you will not need a wedding dress ever again.

The most important thing after the wedding is to make sure that you love and cherish one another, as you deserve. The two of you should look forward to the rest of your lives spent together, as loving husband and wife.

About the Author

Karly Valentine is a professional wedding consultant and a specialist in the weddings and events management industry. She helps bring your day to reality with a minimum of stress for the bride and groom. She has over 17 years of experience coordinating elegant weddings and events. She regularly writes on wedding and event planning and provides expert advice.

Printed in Great Britain
by Amazon

78137900R00149